Playground Personalities

Xulon Press
2301 Lucien Way #415
Maitland, FL 32751
407.339.4217

www.xulonpress.com

© 2021 by Dorice Woodruff

All rights reserved solely by the author. The author guarantees all contents are original and do not infringe upon the legal rights of any other person or work. No part of this book may be reproduced in any form without the written permission of the author. The views expressed in this book are not necessarily those of the publisher.

Due to the changing nature of the Internet, if there are any web addresses, links, or URLs included in this manuscript, these may have been altered and may no longer be accessible. The views and opinions shared in this book belong solely to the author and do not necessarily reflect those of the publisher. The publisher therefore disclaims responsibility for the views or opinions expressed within the work.

Unless otherwise indicated, Scripture quotations taken from the New King James Version (NKJV). Copyright © 1982 by Thomas Nelson, Inc. Used by permission. All rights reserved.

Unless otherwise indicated, Scripture quotations taken from the Holy Bible, New International Version (NIV). Copyright © 1973, 1978, 1984, 2011 by Biblica, Inc.™. Used by permission. All rights reserved.

Unless otherwise indicated, Scripture quotations taken from the English Standard Version (ESV). Copyright © 2001 by Crossway, a publishing ministry of Good News Publishers. Used by permission. All rights reserved.

An effort was made to locate sources of information and quotes when required. If any errors were made to locate copyright holders, it is without malice and deeply regretted.

Cover design by COSMO BARBATO, www.CosmoCreativeStudios.com

For more information, contact:

Dorice Woodruff, DARing People, www.daring-people.com

Printed in the United States of America

Paperback ISBN-13: 978-1-6628-3760-9
Ebook ISBN-13: 978-1-6628-3761-6

Acknowledgments

This book is dedicated to many people who have significantly impacted my life:

- Pastor George Westlake, Sheffield Family Life Center, Kansas City, MO. If I had not encountered your teachings in 1986, I do not know where I would be. You are indeed a vessel of God.

- My mother, Joyce Butts. You have been the only person to be my true rock. Thank you for going out of your way to try to protect me, for your love, your tenacity, and for literally sacrificing everything to raise your children. I am incredibly grateful to be your daughter. I have watched you overcome many physical illnesses and ailments, but you just keep fighting because you are so resilient. You are my hero.

- My husband, James Woodruff, Jr., Thank you for listening to me and pushing me to complete this book. Thank you for your daily prayers when I was in very dark places. Thank you for being my friend and my husband.

- My son, MarVon Smith, Sr., you are a child whose life started with struggle because your destiny is great. I pray that you cultivate your relationship with Jesus Christ, our Lord and Savior and that you become all you are destined to be. Thank you for making my life worth living and for my three beautiful grandchildren.

- My sustainers: Mark Johnson, Desiree Crawl, William Preston Hardrict, Tracie Hardin, Shawn Moore, and James Ware. Thank you for helping to sustain me when God placed it on your heart to do so and for giving without malice or expectation.

- My sister, Patrice Koonce, and my brother, Shelton Butts, Sr., I wish you nothing but happiness. Thank you for your lessons and support at times as well.

- My brother Warren Koonce and maternal grandmother Irma Koonce. I miss and love you. Rest in Heaven. My stepfather, Jay Butts. Rest in Heaven. I did not appreciate you when I was young, but as an adult, I understand the battles you faced. PTSD is real. Thank you for stepping up and doing your best for us.

- The three Servant Leaders that have blessed me:
    - Nancy Lally (Chicago), you are the epitome of

a Servant Leader. You lead with love and heart. You extended your support to me as a person, not just as my boss. You deserve so many great things because of all the love you have shown others. I am blessed to have been one of the recipients of your love and support.

- Joyce Tapley (Dallas), I have never met anyone as authentic as you. Working with you as my CEO was a daily reminder of what it means to lead with heart. Thank you for allowing me to grow professionally and to marry ministry with love for the community.

- John Wells (Chicago), you stand on God's principles even when you stand alone. I appreciate the example you provided and for your willingness to see life through the eyes of others. God has great things in store for you. I hope to see you on a political ballot soon.

- To the interns and professionals that God put in my path to mentor. You have been a blessing and have, in many ways, mentored me as well. I am grateful to see you all moving forward in your lives and careers.

- To John Anthony Fox, my friend since kindergarten. Thank you for reading my manuscript and re-dedicating your life to Christ before leaving this earth six months later. Your transformation was evident, and I am grateful God allowed me to coach you to understanding the true meaning of forgiveness.

Preface

---※---

First and foremost, I want to convey that this book is not a "self-help" or "how to be a better leader" type, although there will be information provided that may serve that purpose. This book is about real-life experiences, observations, and people I have encountered on my professional journey. It is also about God opening my eyes to view ministry in a very unorthodox manner, outside of the physical church building.

In the corporate world, organizations of all sizes, private, public, and non-profit have ministry opportunities awaiting God's people. I am one of those people who learned over time that God was using me in the workplace. I witnessed petty workplace games, people who hurt other people, exalted themselves, lied, created chaotic situations, battled with addictions, and other things. The names, faces, places, and scenarios were different but there was a pattern of wrongdoing and childish behaviors. I will not name anyone or where I encountered them because it is never about people, as I understand that people are not the problem. The Bible says:

> "For we do not wrestle against flesh and blood, but against principalities, against powers, against the rulers of the darkness of this age, against spiritual hosts of wickedness in the heavenly places." Ephesians 6:12 NKJV

The enemy comes to steal, kill, and destroy. What that has meant in my life is the enemy comes to steal my joy, kill my dreams, and destroy my destiny. He has seemingly worked overtime in my life and some of those experiences are outlined in this book. I believe that I have a responsibility to share these experiences to help others understand that they cannot expect people to behave in a way that they feel is adult-like or acceptable. Also, they cannot make people like, accept, or respect them. Remember, there are spiritual forces behind the people that attack us. Every experience, both personal or through observation, ultimately will work out for our greater good and should be viewed as training ground. This training has and will continue to prepare us for the next level. Training will also catapult us to our destiny if we learn and apply the lessons.

> "And we know that all things work together for good to those who love God, to those who are the called according to His purpose. For whom He foreknew, He also predestined to be conformed to the image of His son that he might be the firstborn among many brethren.

Preface

Moreover, whom He predestined, these He also called; whom He called, these He also justified; and whom He justified, these He also glorified." Romans 8:28-30 NKJV

As a child, I witnessed behaviors that were not becoming to some of the children I went to school with. Those behaviors stayed with most of them from grade school to high school. During high school, I thought that as we got older, they would grow out of the destructive behaviors that were so unattractive to their character, but some never did. They just got bigger and older, and for some of them, their behavior got uglier.

Post high school, I held on to the hope that as they went on to adulthood, they would change and act more grown-up, but again, some never did. This made me ask, "How can someone live, grow into adulthood, go through college, get jobs, get married, and have children, yet continue to behave as children?" I thought that somewhere along the line and with a certain age, we were automatically given a measure of maturity and logical reasoning that transformed into more favorable and adult-like behaviors. I do not know why I thought that or where it came from but nonetheless, it was an expectation. Because of this expectation, I have been disappointed and often mortified at some of the ridiculous behavior that I have seen in adults. I have also been disheartened to learn that people do not necessarily grow into responsible, respectable human beings and sometimes they get worse with age. The phrase "some people grow old, but never grow up" is absolutely true. Unbeknownst to me, this phrase did not just apply to people from my childhood, but to people I encountered throughout my life. People from all walks of life to include some of my professors, managers, and other authoritative figures. Year after year, I would meet people with behavioral similarities of those I had encountered in grade school, hence the premise for the title of this book, "Playground Personalities".

Table of Contents

---※---

Introduction vii
Chapter 1: My Journey........................ 1
Chapter 2: Basic Human Tendencies............ 13
Chapter 3: The Struggle is Real.............. 17
Chapter 4: Discipline, Our Daily Exercise ... 23
Chapter 5: The Cast of Characters............ 27
Chapter 6: All Organizations Speak.
    What Does Yours Say? 75
Chapter 7: Can I Be Honest? 93
Chapter 8: Organizational Observations: 101
Chapter 9: What Guides You? 113
Chapter 10: Dealing with the Root Cause,
    Not the Manifestation 117
Summary...................................... 123
Final Word................................... 127

Chapter 1

My Journey

And you will be My witnesses – both in Jerusalem and in Judea and Samaria and as far to the last place of the earth." Acts 1:8 NKJV

As a child, I always felt I was different. Not because I was not popular or accepted, but because I knew at a young age (around four) that there was more to me than my physical or outer presence. I knew there was a realm that we could not see, and it was not just because of the stories that my grandmother would tell, but because I felt it. My grandmother was a faithful Christian, a woman of God who demonstrated servanthood to the Lord Jesus Christ, who left a legacy of fighting battles in the spirit realm. Some of my family members learned at early ages that they had strong spiritual gifts. I did not understand it until I was seventeen years old, a pregnant teenager dying from respiratory-related illnesses. This was where my spiritual journey with a genuine God became personal.

Playground Personalities

Before I go into the moment that I heard the Holy Spirit personally, allow me to tell you about the experiences that paved the way.

For the first three years of my life, I lived with my extended family. My maternal grandmother moved from St. Louis to Kansas City with her two daughters and one of their close friends. My mom (Joyce) had three children, my aunt (Johnnie) had two, and Carol had one. We had a small loving family. Then, my mother got married, and we moved out of the family home into a small house with my stepfather and my younger brother was born.

It seemed like a natural transition because I did not have a relationship with my biological father and did not know him at that time. I met my father when I was six. He came to Kansas City to gather my sister and me to spend two weeks in Saint Louis, Missouri, with him and his new wife. I was so depressed, and this was the longest trip of my life. I longed to be home with my mother and not these strangers. I never felt loved or wanted by my biological father. That feeling never changed, although I tried for many years to get to know him. He passed on in 2012, and I did not feel anything except lost opportunities. He was an acquaintance to me, not a father, and I could not make myself feel any differently.

When I was a young child, I guess around eight to nine years of age, I seemed to fret about everything. I was filled with anxiety because I really did not have a strong prayer life. We were Easter, Mother's Day, and Christmas Christians. I did not know half the things said in church, but I always felt there was something more significant and substantial than us (human beings). I used to stare in the mirror for long periods and ask questions like, "How did I get here?" "Why do my spirit and my body feel disconnected?" "Why do I care so much for people?" "Why don't they care more?" "How can people hurt each other?" My siblings used to call me strange because I would sit in the closet of my room and read or write in my journal. We had a small house that six people lived in. I shared a room with my sister, who was four years older. It was really her room and her rules; I was just allowed to be in it. The only peace I had was when I was over my grandmother's or in the closet.

At the age of ten I witnessed my stepfather having Delirium Tremens (DT's). He was suffering from PTSD (Post Traumatic Stress Disorder) from the Vietnam War but was not aware of it. He started shaking, sweating, and reliving the war. He was throwing people on the floor, hiding when someone knocked on the door, and saying that the neighbor's kids were hiding under his bed. This was awkward behavior because he was not intoxicated at the time this occurred. We were used to him throwing up, fighting, cussing, joking, dancing, falling asleep outside in the grass, and even urinating in other parts of the house that were not the bathroom when he was intoxicated. As I said, he was an extremely heavy drinker. But this day, I knew something was terribly wrong. So that night, I put a butcher knife under my pillow and tried to sleep. But, of course, I did not get any sleep because anxiety would not let me. The next day my siblings and I went to school as usual. As odd as it may sound, I was awaiting some bad news. I could not enjoy school, my friends, or even pay attention that day because I was watching the clock and waiting on the news. My younger brother and I were called over the school intercom to the office for early release. Our Aunt Theresia picked us up and took us home where my sister and older brother were waiting. Our older siblings said he had been picked up, put in a straight-jacket, and taken to the VA Hospital. I did not know what detox and mental wards meant, but I knew that he was gone for several weeks and during this time I slept peacefully. No anxiety. There was no drinking, parties, or fights in my home for the first time in years. Peace finally filled the atmosphere.

At thirteen years of age, I realized that my mother was self-medicating with alcohol too. She did not drink hard liquor, but she drank beer every day. She seemed depressed, but like many African American people, she did not go to the doctor or believe in any mental health help. My stepfather was drinking heavily again and lost another good job. By this time, both my older sister and brother had moved out. My mother allowed me too much freedom and, as you would imagine, it was a recipe for disaster. I stopped taking my education seriously in my sophomore year of high school. Worst of all, I got involved with a guy who was five years my senior and abusive emotionally and physically. I thought I was in love because, after all, I did not really know what healthy love looked like. The day I decided to leave him was when he knocked me down a flight of stairs at his friend's house. Granted, I had been beaten by him before in the two years I dated him, but not like this. He was performing for his friend, who was also an abuser of women. He busted my lip and was I bleeding from my mouth. He did not care because he was trying to prove his manhood to his friend. He came down the stairs and beat me up so badly that all I could do was pray because my begging him to stop and crying was only making matters worse. I whispered to God, "If you get me out of this one, I will never put myself in this predicament again!" I got away from him and walked home. The distance was about twenty-four miles. It was a cold fall night, and I was alone, walking through bad neighborhoods at sixteen. I was so angry that I was not bothered by the long walk or the dangers that surrounded me. I did not feel the cold or my bodily pain. I just felt overwhelmed with feelings of anger from being betrayed, used, and hurt.

By my senior year in high school, I was a pregnant teen. I was so lonely during my pregnancy because most of my high school friends shunned me. One true friend, Kristie, invited me to her church, which was the day I got saved.

Sheffield Family Life Center, under the direction of Pastor George Westlake, had a play they did every year between Thanksgiving and Christmas called Tribulation Christmas. It was about the Rapture and what life would be like for those left on Earth during the seven years of tribulation. I had not ever experienced any church like this before. When the play ended, Pastor Westlake spoke, and it was so powerful that God's Word set that place on fire. For the first time, I observed the gifts of the spirit, such as speaking in tongues, interpreting of tongues, and prophesying. What really intrigued me was that I saw a known prostitute (I knew of her from roller-skating) go to the altar and accept Christ. I was amazed because no one shunned her or gave her disapproving looks, although she was dressed provocatively. This was different from other churches I observed in the past. I knew if they could accept her, they could accept me too, a pregnant teenager. So, I walked up to the altar, and this is where my relationship went from the occasional prayer or church visit on holidays to having a thirsting and hunger for God's Word and presence.

God's timing was impeccable because a week after I got Saved, I was hospitalized with asthma, bronchitis, and pneumonia. I was seven and one-half months pregnant when I got to the hospital and was there for weeks. They kept me sedated most of the time because my right lung was at the point of collapse. They had to keep me from going into labor because I could not deliver naturally due to my lung capacity. I woke up one day and heard two nurses talking. I opened my eyes, and one of them approached me urgently as I was trying to take the tubes out of my nose. She put something in my IV, and instantly I was asleep again. Another time I woke up, and a Chaplain was in the room with me, praying over me. I tried to remain inconspicuous because I did not want him to have the nurses put me to sleep again. I listened to his prayer. I then got up out of bed and walked on his right side. I felt I could sneak past him since he was praying so earnestly. I was trying to get to my mother because I heard her voice outside my hospital room. On my way to the door, I realized that the weight in my belly was not there, I was significantly lighter, and my feet were not touching the floor. I looked down at my stomach and I was not pregnant. I immediately panicked because I thought I had lost the baby. I looked back at the bed and saw my pregnant body lying there with tubes and machines. At this point, it was as though I could hear my mother in stereo talking to the doctor. I then listened to a booming male voice say, "Go! Lay back on your body, pray and ask God for what you want!" I immediately complied as instructed. My prayer specifically was that God would allow me to live to see my son. The next day that same Chaplain came to my room to pray for me, and he seemed perplexed. I told him I was hungry and wanted lasagna. I thanked him for praying over me the night before, and he said, "You can't possibly know I was here because you were sedated." I responded and told him what he was wearing and what he was saying in his prayer. He stuck around for a short while, but as medical staff entered and exited, it became chaotic because they were also perplexed. That day I went from 1500 MG of Theophylline to none. My lungs were clear, and I was breathing on my own, no machines or tubes. I was immediately and miraculously healed and released from the hospital the following day.

I returned two weeks later to deliver my son in January of 1987. A few hours after delivery, I began to hemorrhage after I saw and held my son. Large clots of blood filled my bed pad. I got up to walk to the bathroom, and blood clots the size of my hand fell out of me and burst on the floor. I was weak at the point of fainting. When the nurses were alerted, I had to have a D&C (Dilatation and Curettage) and a blood transfusion. At that time, that same dismal feeling that life was leaving my body came back to me. I remembered praying and asking God to let me live to see my son. This time, I prayed again and asked God to let me live to raise my son, see him become the man God wants him to be, and let me fulfill the destiny for my life. My healing happened immediately and miraculously again. The next day I was released from the hospital with restrictions.

I did not know that God was showing me that He equipped me with the gift of Intercessory Prayer, a gift that would feel like a burden from that point forward until I surrendered. Another God-given gift was the gift of Discernment.

My Journey

I possessed the ability to see things I could not explain (some things I did not want to see), feel the emotions that people were hiding, feel unseen energy, smell spiritual forces, and dream or visualize things before they happened.

Despite all that God had shown me and allowed me to live through, I still rebelled. Not blatantly, but gradually. I was weak and recovering from the problems I experienced during my pregnancy and delivery in 1987. Still, by 1989, I was back to being an avid roller-skater, and that experience of fighting for my life was becoming a distant memory, as was my relationship with the Lord. By 1991, I found another worldly distraction, the nightclub. I barely, if at all, attended church after 1988. I was drifting more and more into a life where my love for God was on the backburner until the Holy Spirit allowed me to see what I had opened myself to, with all my partying and dating the wrong men.

One night in 1991, my friends and I were preparing for our regular "Ladies Night" on Thursday nights at a Lounge in Kansas City. Every week, we had cocktails and got ready at my apartment. We knew we would be surrounded by men who made their money in questionable ways and a few of the city's football players. I sat at my dressing table to apply make-up, and as I looked into the mirror, a murky gray-greenish color flushed my skin. Initially, I stepped away, cleansed my face again, and sat down to reapply my make-up. Once again, that ugly color embellished my skin. The only way I can describe it would be similar to that of the Wicked Witch of the West from The Wizard of Oz. I immediately jumped away from my dressing table because it frightened me. As I did this, I heard the Holy Spirit say, "This is what you look like inside." At that point, I cried and listened to Him speak more. Finally, he said, "This is not the reason you asked for your life to be preserved!" I was overcome with feelings of shame and grief because I knew I had abandoned God, and He was not pleased with my lifestyle. I never made it to the club that night, and from that day forward, I started making the changes necessary to live better and focus on my relationship with the Lord, who preserved my life four years earlier.

Like Jonah in the Bible, I went off rebelliously at times trying to make my own agendas more important than the mandates of God. I have tried to avoid the assignments that were confirmed for me. I have attempted not to deliver messages that God told me to give, and I suffered greatly. When I did accept the assignments from God, I was not always received with open arms but walking in his purpose makes it easier. Even though the lessons came with much pain, the growth was well-worth it. The Bible said we would be a "peculiar people," which has held true in my life.

But ye are a chosen generation, a royal priesthood, an holy nation, a peculiar people; that ye should shew forth praises of him who hath called you out of darkness into his marvelous light. 1 Peter 2:9 NKJV

All of God's chosen people are unique no matter what office of the Five-Fold Ministry they operate from or what spiritual gifts with which they are equipped.

And He Himself gave some to be apostles, some prophets, some evangelists, and some pastors and teachers for the equipping of the saints for the work of ministry, for the edifying of the body of Christ, till we all come to the unity of the faith and knowledge of the Son of God, to a perfect man, to the measure of the stature of the fullness of Christ. Ephesians 4: 11-13 NKJV

I do not profess to be a Bible scholar and will therefore not attempt to break down the meaning, mantle, or the attributes required for each office because that is not the purpose of this book. I have had the office of a Prophet confirmed for me, and that is not the office I wanted because Prophets suffer, experience tremendous warfare, and are targets for spiritual and physical attacks. That confirmation made the incidents of my life comprehensible.

Chapter 2

Basic Human Tendencies

I have been blessed to be a student of life. God has allowed me to live in different cities and to observe how people behave. I have seen cultures divided into many sub-cultures by socioeconomic status, race, religion, gender, and other factors. The social norms and values have changed as it pertains to what is and is not acceptable in American standards. Historical events, radical groups, and politicians seem to shape our view of the world at large.

Despite all these factors, I have watched and learned that there are three basic groups of people in the physical world. Explorers, Settlers, and Followers. I use these words to describe human behavior in almost every situation known to man. Our civilization was built upon them, and each group is necessary.

Explorers – These are the people who do not allow fear to stop them from stepping out and taking a chance at

Playground Personalities

discovering what is outside of their norm. These are your risk-takers, trailblazers, and pioneers. They seem to embrace change quickly and are always looking for the next new thing. They pride themselves on discoveries and innovation. They have a broader perspective of thinking, for their motto is "courage is not the absence of fear, but action in the face of fear."

In organizations, Explorers usually hold management roles because they are natural leaders. This is just a part of who they are.

Settlers — These are the people that get comfortable and stay in that place of comfort, even if that place becomes uncomfortable. They take pride in being sticklers of longevity. You will be able to identify your settlers because they have been in the same places and businesses for long periods and usually resist change. They reminisce on how things used to be, wishing that the glory days could return. They may not necessarily be growing in their ability to see things from different perspectives, but they are great at keeping traditions. Their motto is, "We have always done it this way."

In organizations, Settlers may hold management roles or roles of individual contributors. They are not always natural leaders, but the skillset of management can be developed. These are the people in your organizations who will resist changes unless they make perfect sense, as risk-taking is not a part of their genetic make-up. Anything that throws them out of their comfort zones or causes them to have to adjust to different things, especially drastic changes, will put them in a place of fear.

Followers — These are the people who either do not have a natural yearning to be an Explorer or Settler, but they choose to follow one or the other. They do not have a strong propensity to take a stand for what they believe in and usually like to follow someone they admire or identify with. They will learn and grow, but usually because of who they are attached to. Their motto seems to be "I am very loyal to the people I love and find my identity in them."

In organizations, Followers will hold all types of roles because, as stated, they tend to mimic or follow those people they admire. Those people can be Explorers or Settlers.

All three groups of people are necessary for shaping our cultures, organizations, cities, towns, and churches. Without Explorers, everything would stay the same and never evolve. I feel that evolution is necessary and those things that do not evolve will eventually become extinct. Without Settlers, valuable traditions and tried-true methods would be lost, and there would be no familiarity of what has been or has worked. Without Followers, Explorers would have no one to lead and Settlers would have no community.

Playground Personalities

Each one has its good and bad points, and you will be able to identify them all in this book.

Time to Reflect

- Are you an Explorer, a Settler, or a Follower?
- Have there been situations that defined this for you?
- Has that changed over a period of time?
- Does your work environment or culture depict the group you fall into?

Chapter 3

The Struggle is Real

I do not understand what I do. For what I want to do, I do not do, but what I hate to do. And if I do what I do not want to do, I agree that the law is good. As it is, it is no longer I who do it, but it is sin living in me. For I know that good itself does not dwell in me, that is, in my sinful nature. Romans 7:15-18 NKJV

In addition to the three groupings of exploring, settling, and following, I believe we have natural desires and things that we are attracted to. Some of these things will keep us from living right and doing the will of God. When it comes to people, there is good and bad because people are extremely complex creatures who encompass a mind, body, and spirit. Some behaviors and desires will be mild and infrequent, other things may be reoccurring themes, and some behaviors or desires may be just plain disturbing. The Bible says:

For all that is in the world – the lust of the flesh, the desire of the eye and pride of life is not of the Father but is of the world. 1 John 2:16 NKJV

We are made from the dust of the earth and to earth we shall return. We, therefore, are attracted to the things of this earth. Have you ever wondered why good things take longer to obtain and require discipline to hold on to? Think about it, bad habits start quickly and progress before we ever have a chance to get them under control.

There is always the infamous debate of nature versus nurture in developing our habits, traits, and personalities. I do not know which one truly defines a person. Still, I will go as far as to say that looking at nature (genetics and what we inherit through our bloodlines) and nurture (what we inherit from our upbringing and influences), the two work simultaneously to form our flesh man (mind and body). The Holy Spirit in us is battling these influences to give us Godly character so that we can fulfill our destiny.

Being a person that has had to fight the battle of the bulge, I realize that food has been my struggle and my drug of choice. Nothing better than a piece of cake on those days that I am stressed. Before I realized it, I was thirty pounds overweight and dealing with high blood pressure. It has been many years, and I still struggle with fasting food and keeping my flesh in submission. Everyone struggles with something, and I am honest enough to tell what my struggles are. This habit of eating sweets was not developed overnight. Oh no, it started incredibly early in life in my daily runs to the candy store or when I would save my lunch money to purchase chocolate and taffy from the candy-pusher at school. It did not seem like a problem at that time because I was active and petite.

Eating junk food was my habit (what I developed through nurture), but high blood pressure was the consequence (what I inherited through nature). All this to say, behaviors are set and do not change until we consciously change them or battle with the consequences of nature. When we learn that we cannot change habits and behaviors on our own, we have to give it to God and pray to be delivered from these things. Would I say that junk food is a stronghold for me? Absolutely. A stronghold that started innocently and progressed over time. I have to go cold-turkey on sweets because the Bible says:

A little leaven leavens a whole lump. Galatians 5:9 NKJV

This means, when I open the door and start consuming sweets, I am up ten pounds and wondering how I let this happen. The lust of my eye in seeing the cake triggered the lust of my flesh to want to taste the cake, and the pride of life was me telling myself I could handle it, and I had it under control.

Playground Personalities

My struggle is desserts and sweets. Other people may struggle with drugs, gambling, sex, gossiping, cursing, lying, and other things. I have had to personally overcome gossiping, cursing and other sinful things. Therefore, this is a judgement-free zone. I am merely stating we have to know and acknowledge our struggles to control them. We also have to see them as sin and not try to justify them. That which we fail to control will eventually control us. Our habits and behaviors start subtly. The more we allow ourselves to have these bad habits, outbursts, or displays, the more we will justify it as okay. So, we go from being out of control children to out of control adults. Think about it, no one starts smoking marijuana with hopes of becoming a full-fledged drug addict, living under a bridge, or sitting on the street corner begging for money. No one plays cards with family and friends with hopes of being a gambler who loses their home or children's college funds. No one takes a drink with hopes of becoming the town drunk. No one has sex with the hopes of becoming the neighborhood loosy-goosy. No one eats junk food with the hopes of being on My 600 Pound Life. No one starts hunting animals or playing video games with shooting and killing with hopes of becoming the next notorious serial killer. What is worse is that most of these habits have been seen and despised by the people struggling with them throughout their family history. Yes, the behaviors children witness will sometimes become the behaviors they perpetuate.

Time to Reflect

- What are some things that you have struggled with again and again?

- What are the habits that you need to put behind you to live a life pleasing to God?

- Did nature or nurture develop your habit?

- Do you know the consequences if you don't stop the habit?

- Are you prepared to deal with the consequences if you don't?

Chapter 4

Discipline, Our Daily Exercise

Therefore, having been justified by faith, we have peace with God through our Lord Jesus Christ, through whom also we have access by faith into grace in which we stand and rejoice in hope of the glory of God. And not only that, but we also glory in tribulations, knowing that tribulation produces perseverance; and perseverance character; and character, hope. Romans 5:1-4. NKJV

Living a disciplined life requires a lot from us. As I said, bad habits are easy to develop, but the result of them can be detrimental. Good habits are harder to develop, but their effect is beneficial. I always think about the statement, "no pain, no gain." This is so true. Getting our fleshly desires under submission and developing good habits is a daily mental, physical and spiritual exercise. We must stay plugged into our power source, Jesus Christ, with prayer and keeping our mind fixated upon him.

Playground Personalities

Everything starts with the state of our minds and decisions. What we allow ourselves to think will determine our behaviors and perceptions. So daily discipline begins with positive thoughts. Three scriptures really are relevant to disciplining our thoughts:

- *For out of the abundance of the heart, the mouth speaks. Matthew 12:34. NKJV*

- *Death and life are in the power of the tongue, and those who love it will eat its fruit. Proverbs 18:21. NKJV*

- *As a man thinketh in his heart, so is he. Proverbs 23:7. NKJV*

Just like our physical bodies, when we stop practicing good habits, the old ones resurface stronger, and the natural consequences are more severe. We find ourselves feeling bad about letting things get out of control and attempt to get back to practicing good habits. The more we feed the flesh, the harder we battle. We find it challenging to be consistent in our practices, and the results seem to be shorter. The reason for this is based on this scripture:

When an unclean spirit goes out of a man, he goes through dry places, seeking rest, and finds none. Then he says, I will return to my house from which I came. And when he comes, he finds it empty, swept, and put

in order. Then he goes and takes with him seven other spirits more wicked than himself, and they enter and dwell there; and the last state of that man is worse than the first. So shall it also be with this wicked generation.
Matthew 12:43-45 NKJV

It is essential to exercise obedience and discipline daily to maintain what we have overcome. If we do not, it will manifest again, and we will have more problems than initially. I can attest to the yo-yo dieting that I have done for years. Each time it gets more challenging mentally, physically, and spiritually. Each time I have more weight to lose, and health problems have surfaced as a result.

For example, think of a habit as a spiritual problem, a demon that has attached itself to you like a parasite. You feed this small demon parasite and it becomes a bigger demon parasite that eventually takes vitamins and nutrients from your body until it depletes you. You get rid of the demon parasite but fail to fill your body with the proper nutrients (God's word) to ward off that demon parasite and other ones like it. The demon parasite has survived for eons and has no sense of time, so it waits for you to drop your guard and open the door for it to return. This demon parasite returns with seven more demon parasites that are stronger and deadlier than the one you had. Your battle now is greater.

Therefore, submit to God. Resist the devil and he will flee from you. James 4:7 NKJV

Time to Reflect

- What areas in your life need better discipline?
- Is obedience or rebellion a problem for you?
- Have you tried to stop a habit before and when you opened yourself back up to the problem, it was more difficult to stop?
- Did you ask God for help?
- Are you willing to fast along with prayer? Some things require fasting and prayer.

Chapter 5

The Cast of Characters

In this chapter, I will detail some of things I have observed or experienced dealing with people in workplaces. Some were spiritually sick, some emotionally wounded, some just sinister, and others filled with the seven deadly sins which are lust, pride, greed, gluttony, envy, slothfulness, and wrath. Remember, there are spiritual influences in the behaviors of these people. As mentioned in Chapter 3, you will see the Explorers, Settlers, and Followers in these examples of Playground Personalities. Here are some of the characters I have met on my journey.

The Attention Seeker

The Attention Seeker has an appetite for more because nothing satisfies them for long periods. They do not have a clue that the world does not revolve around them. Their hunger is not just about material things but also includes people and favor. These people want everyone to admire, cater to, and envy them at the same time.

In the workplace, the attention seeker desires to be the center of attention and envied by everyone. They thrive on any form of attention, even negative attention, and will get it by any means necessary. Attention Seekers have difficulty getting along with others because they are too self-centered to see that they are the common denominator to their problems with so many people.

I once worked with someone who slept her way to the top with men in powerful positions, both inside of companies and outside. She was outwardly beautiful; therefore, a lot of her ugly behavior was overlooked by men. She often bragged about having children by millionaires and dating famous men. From the outside looking in, she had everything materially one could ask for; a good job, a famous boyfriend, children by wealthy men who were paying her handsomely, nice cars, a beautiful expensive home, and the ability to travel whenever and wherever she wanted. She was extremely hateful toward certain women. Any woman who was educated, good-looking, and well-groomed automatically became her competitor and enemy because they were threats to her limelight, and she was not sharing it.

She ran the women off who got attention from the men in the office. She was the reason for so much turnover in

The Cast Of Characters

the workplace because she held the second-highest role in this small company. I am pretty sure she had no idea how much she was costing this operation, and based on her actions, she probably would not care if she was made aware because her focus was not the company, it was herself! She was plagued by the deadly sin of pride that manifested as vanity.

I also worked with another man who used his illnesses and ailments to get attention. He was a hefty man who was classified as legally blind. Although his eyesight was minimal, he did not require a service animal.

He would frequently come into our Human Resources offices to have people waiting on him hand and foot when he was supposed to be working. He would talk for hours about his illnesses while the young ladies in Human Resources fetched him water and candy bars and entertained his need to be noticed. I realized very quickly that he was an Attention Seeker who had apparently been doing this for years. I always felt an undercurrent of perversion in him, and my flesh would crawl when he was present. He would brag about how the Executives had given him certificates to get free meals and other company benefits before my arrival. When I became the Director, I would politely ask him if he was on the clock and his business in the Human Resources department. I quickly put a stop to his one-hour on-the-clock breaks that he would take

Playground Personalities

visiting the women in HR.

Of course, he did not like me very much and was out for revenge because I stopped his games and did not feed is need for attention. One evening, after regular business hours, he entered HR to file a complaint. It was not uncommon for me to stay late to assist managers and employees on later shifts. I typed his complaint verbatim as he spoke it. He stated that some of our male employees had come into the locker room the night before and told him to suck their big male private parts (of course that is not the verbiage that was given). This seemed unbelievable, so I stopped typing and looked up at him. What caught my attention immediately was the way his private part was jumping. He continued to repeat it as if he were enjoying saying it to me. Remember, he was an enormous man who barely fit in the seat, so he would have to lean back into the chair, pushing his hip area forward. I pressed the panic button inconspicuously, waiting for a security officer. I began to distract him by asking the color of their uniforms, what their voices sounded like, and what time it was. When the second shift security supervisor arrived, I asked him to repeat his story in the presence of the male security officer, but he refused. He sat straight up in the seat and said, "It is so vulgar that I cannot repeat it!" I read back the statement to him with the witness present and pointed out the fact that he had no problem saying it to me alone. I told him we would look into it and dismissed him from my office. I immediately explained to the security supervisor what I had witnessed when I was alone with the Attention Seeker. We ran security footage for the night before and several other nights only to learn that no one entered the locker room when he was there. I went back into the Employee Relations files, and two years prior, he had been written-up for being on his cell phone having phone sex in the locker room. It was overheard by some male co-workers and reported to Human Resources. When we brought him back into the HR office three days later. I informed him that his complaint could not be substantiated, and he started asking me to look back earlier that week. I told him we had reviewed security footage the day of his complaint and fourteen days prior, and nothing he stated was true. I warned him that filing false complaints was against company policy and explained that his complaint was similar to his previous write-up. I also informed him that he seemed aroused when he told me the story before the arrival of the male security supervisor. He swore he was telling the truth, although we both knew he was lying. He was lustful and perverse and therefore, enjoyed saying those vulgar things to me when he had me alone.

A couple of weeks later, he was suspended for something else he had done on the job and called me on the phone, stating that he would commit suicide if I terminated him. I told him that I was dispatching the police to his home for a wellness check. He begged me not to, but I informed him I had a duty to do this. That was also a hoax. Another opportunity to gain attention and attempt to manipulate me like he had done so many in the past. He then told the Union Shop Stewards that I was out to get him fired. I met with them and provided factual information about my interactions with him. After speaking with me, they told him they would not escalate his complaints through the formal grievance process. I did not hear from him again for a while. He later came into HR and faked a fainting episode when he was caught in another situation involving his behavior on the job. Again, this guy would not stop at anything to get the attention he wanted so badly.

But for those who are self-seeking and who reject the truth and follow evil, there will be wrath and anger.
Romans 2:8 NIV

The Awkward Intimidator

The Awkward Intimidator is the person who seemingly lack social skills and does not fit in with the kids in school. Their nonverbal communication indicates that they are unsure of themselves because they do not make eye contact and avoid verbal communication. These people often have imaginary friends when they are young. They do not mesh with their peers and are therefore aloof. They may be brilliant, but no one takes time to know because they are not good communicators face-to-face. Their lack of verbal expression in childhood sometimes transcends to visual or creative expression in adolescence as they rebel against the status quo. Sometimes their writing and drawings disturb their teachers, or they dress in a manner that solidifies their inability or unwillingness to assimilate. Whatever form of chosen expression, it comes from a place of hurt that stem from years of trauma and rejection.

An incident stands out to me regarding the social awkwardness of a guy who started emailing a young lady at work about business, but the emails oddly progressed. He would send her emails acting as though he had reciprocal dialogue with her. She always remained professional and only responded to the business aspects of his emails. After a short while, she stopped responding to his emails altogether. She was truly kind and ignored his advances hoping he would stop. Finally, after about six months of odd emails wishing her a wonderful day, telling her to be careful going home, or telling her about the weather outside, he decided to try to talk to her in person. He approached her during open enrollment for benefits and asked her a personal question about who she lives with. She told him she lived with her boyfriend, hoping it would stop his interest in her. He left the enrollment meeting and then followed up in the email. He scared her because he threatened to kill her if she lied to him again. He told her he knew she did not live with her boyfriend and only lived with her young son. She gathered the emails and put them in date order for investigation. After reading the six-month stack of daily emails, I recognized a pattern of frequent communication where he was clearly having an imaginary relationship with her. It was apparent that he had been physically and cyberstalking her and her child. Who knows how that story would have ended had she not spoken up? Lifetime movies are made behind things like this. I was the unfortunate investigator that had to interview this guy about the disturbing emails and to let him know he was being terminated. I saw him go from being quiet and squeamish to yelling and grabbing his hair with both hands. He was extremely uncomfortable with me reading his messages back to him. It looked like I was torturing him with the truth. Finally, he jumped up and reached over my desk, trying to grab me. I pushed the chair back and yelled for help. He was unaware that two state officers were outside of my office, waiting to present the restraining order and question him about the stalking.

That guy had some major psychological issues, which are really spiritual issues of demonic oppression, influence, or possession. Negative emotions from trauma and rejection attract these things.

Then His fame went throughout all Syria; and they brought to Him all sick people who were afflicted with various diseases and torments, and those who were demon possessed, epileptics, and paralytics; and He healed them. Matthew 4:24 NKJV

The Cast Of Characters

The Bully

The Bully is a person that operates from a strong sense of insecurity, and they often display aggressive tendencies. For example, the School Bully was the person who picked on anyone they felt they were physically stronger, bigger, or just more aggressive than. Most of the students were scared of this person because they created an environment of fear and intimidation.

The bad thing about the Bully was that they were not afraid to fight and could usually back up the threats with physical activity, and they were not scared to do it. The Bully was successful at being a bully because most children were taught to get along with others and display manners, which means they were not aggressive or confrontational. Hence, their best course of action was to avoid the Bully. They observed the bully picking on other people but would not intervene because of their fear of being the next target for the Bully. The only way this Bully was stopped was when someone stood up to them and beat them up or when an adult or authoritative figure intervened.

The Workplace Bully is no different as the characteristics are almost identical, but instead of using physical aggression, they use verbal aggression and abuse of power. They take pride in having people who fear them and confuse it with respect. They make people in lower-ranking positions

Playground Personalities

or who are not assertive and confident their target. They will embarrass them in front of their peers or talk to them in a way that assassinates their character or intimidates them. All of the things I have learned about the Workplace Bully states that most are women. This shocked me because I always thought of a bully as a man, and most bullies I encountered were males. But when I finally met the first female Workplace Bully, I have to admit that she was a force to be reckoned with.

She was a large woman in stature and had a high-ranking position as well. She was moody, to say the least. Her mood set the tone for many people that worked in the office with her. If she smiled and said, "Good morning," it was a good day in the office. If she slammed doors and cabinets and did not speak, it was uncomfortable for those in the office. People would literally come in and ask what kind of mood she was in. It was a great day in the office when she was away. It was awful!

She was argumentative, petty, territorial, prideful, and self-centered. Remarkably similar to the character Meryl Streep played on the Devil Wears Prada, a movie that came out in 2006 directed by David Frankel. If someone went around her to get something done or questioned her, they would become her target. She would shun them, talk down to them, and loved doing it in the presence of other people. She could not take any constructive criticism and would lash out at anyone who pointed out anything that she did wrong. People feared her because they never knew when her wrath would come to bite them.

I had a male Bully boss once, and he too was a force to be reckoned with. He was selfish, self-centered, prideful, and would stop at nothing to get what he wanted. He did not value anyone who disagreed with him.

He had a group of false supporters who followed him for fear of losing their job. In my opinion, he would get an "F" if we categorized people by grades. He made it clear that he did not like me because I was black and only hired me because his previous white HR person did not want to relocate with him. He was a Baby Boomer who valued long hours in the office as a measurement of productivity. I am a Gen X-er who does not mind long hours on a project basis, but not as a way of life. He made it clear verbally and, in his behaviors, often in the presence of others, that I was his target. Although people came to me privately to support me, they feared keeping their job, so they said nothing in his presence.

It was common knowledge that he was a raging alcoholic as he would come to work sometimes smelly and disheveled. There were times he offered jobs to people while out drinking and having a good time. These were jobs some of them were not qualified for or had not applied to. In one instance, he hired a young man without doing

Playground Personalities

a background check. After I completed the background check and discovered he was listed as a registered sex offender, I had to rescind the offer because of the nature of our business. This bully boss was so upset with me because he seemed to have a personal attraction and liking for this young man as he did many young, Hispanic men for all the wrong reasons.

Of course, I had to challenge him to keep him honest to avoid lawsuits to the company. He felt that I was overstepping my boundaries by reminding him of the corporate rules for hiring. He was so arrogant, outwardly aggressive, and appalled that I challenged him that he could not see I was trying to protect him and the Company. Finally, after a ten-month battle of extreme warfare, I sent a letter to Corporate Headquarters explaining all the shenanigans he was responsible for. Luckily, a few high-level executives at the corporate level could corroborate portions of my story from what they had witnessed on visits to the office. I was delivered from that battle after standing up to this Goliath.

Before taking this assignment, I was warned by a Prophet to be prepared for this battle. She told me that it would require me to face this demonic entity. It was warfare from the day I assumed the assignment until it was over. In the end, God sent support from a few well-known, outside organizations. After hearing my story and others, these fantastic people stood up for righteousness because his reputation for dealing with his employees was concerning. They fought the final battle after I had been delivered. Even after I was gone, this demonic entity did not stop trying to destroy me.

I did not know many people in that city and that Bully Boss was the only enemy I had. As hard as it is to believe, I know he hired a hitman to either rough me up or kill me. I encountered the guy at Walmart and noticed him following me throughout the store. He was about 5 ft 10 inches tall, white male, reddish brown hair, brown leather jacket, jeans, and work boots. Purposely, I walked into the feminine products aisle, and this is when I knew he was following me deliberately. I spoke loudly to the person I was talking with on the phone and described him to them. He heard me and he was also talking to someone on an earpiece. He stated that he had me right in front of him and asked what they wanted him to do. Apparently, he was given the order to abort his mission at that time. He left the store in a hurry without making a purchase. I followed behind him and went to the store Security guard and pointed out the man as he drove off. I also called the police in that city to explain what I was experiencing and who I felt was responsible. I boarded a plane that same day and left the city for two months with few clothes. I returned for four days to pack my apartment and leave for good. I did not let anyone at that company know I was in town for fear that the hitman would return to complete his mission.

After I left the city permanently, that male bully boss continued to defame my character by giving a negative employment reference. I was turned down for a job after an excellent interview. He also slandered me to people who were mutual colleagues. This was against the company policy and against the severance agreement. I could have sued him personally, but God did not release me to do so. He had a lot of money, pride, and hatred, which was a recipe for spiritual disaster. A wise person once told me that the scariest person in the world is one that does not have anything to lose. While I would agree with that, this situation proved that another one of the scariest people in the world is one that has a lot to lose, and too much pride to have it threatened. He will get his judgment if he does not repent. The Bible says:

He permitted no one to do them wrong; yes, He rebuked kings for their sakes, saying, "Do not touch My anointed ones, and do My prophets no harm. Moreover, He called for a famine in the land; he destroyed all the provision of bread." Psalm 105:14-16. NKJV

The Discord Cultivator

The Discord Cultivator is a person who is usually very likable because they are social butterflies. They approach every new person they encounter and make people comfortable by appearing so down-to-earth, but their real goal is to gain information to use against them. The Discord Cultivator drops embers and sparks that create conflict everywhere they go. They have just enough information to be dangerous, and when they strike, they do a lot of damage because no one suspects them as the culprit. People just keep feeding them information and telling them secrets. When they are pinpointed as the fire starter, it is often too late, and damage is done. In school, you could recognize them because they changed cliques many times due to their inability to be loyal to their friends; therefore, they caused problems with the people they became close to and then switched friends.

I hired a woman once into an administrative role. She came from a job making a meager hourly wage and based on her resume, she was way over-qualified for what she was doing. Within a year after she was hired, she became an exempt professional, making an excellent wage. She was intelligent, friendly, and educated. She talked about how happy she was to be at this company and made friendships with everyone in the organization. Although it is nice to be kind to everyone, she seemed to get close to people I had to discipline or terminate. I could not trust her, which was not good because she worked in Human Resources, a department requiring confidentiality, integrity, and ethics.

When she left my department, she did the same thing to the Executive that hired her as her assistant. I later found

Playground Personalities

out that this woman gossiped about me and others on the Executive team, to include our Chief Executive Officer. She lied and did everything she could to turn people against us. She told people I was her "Judas" as if I was the deceiver and she was the good one. If anything, she was my "Judas." People were happy to see her go when she left the organization because many realized how manipulative and damaging, she was. Even in her last week of work, she continued to gossip and create divisions. All the while, smiling in the faces of the managers she had talked so badly about. She even managed to muster up fake tears and stated how much she loved and would miss us. She caused a lot of problems and then played victim. I have not kept up with her, but one thing for sure is that she has planted many seeds of discord and will eventually reap a harvest of the seeds she has planted.

A worthless person, a wicked man, walks with a perverse mouth; he winks with his eyes, he shuffles his feet, he points with his fingers; perversity is in his heart, he devises evil continually, he sows discord.
Proverbs 6:12-14 NKJV

The Jock

The School Jock is the attractive, athletic, popular guy that all the girls seemed attracted to. He harbored a sense of pride and power because his future seemed promising athletically. Let us face it, most women are attracted to popularity, power, and money. Insecure women are also competitive with other women, so the jock gains status due to the expressed desire from them to be in his world. Movies have often depicted the jock as a "dummy" because he was all athletic and had no brains, but I have seen many jocks with athleticism and academic astuteness. The behaviors that formed in him as a result of his childhood popularity carried over into his adulthood. In college, he was the ever-popular fraternity brother or athlete. In the workplace, he is the Corporate Player.

The "Corporate Player" is charismatic, often in a position of power, and can move someone forward or keep them stagnant in their careers. Unfortunately, most women will become a part of his harem because of his power, popularity, and position. There is no difference between the Jock and the Corporate Player, except his playground went from the school campus to the workplace.

I once worked with a man who held the position of a Sales Director who hired primarily young, inexperienced, attractive women for his sales team. He was a middle-aged married man. We later learned that he had slept with half of his sales team in a four-city region. For those he did not sleep with, he was laying the foundation to do so. He kept a journal of his "sex-capades" on a detachable floppy disc (this was the early 1990's). He would drive throughout his sales territory, wining and dining the beautiful young women who worked under him using company funds. It was discovered because he forgot to detach the disc from a shared computer, and an investigation commenced. He was terminated immediately.

When I learned of his termination, I was reminded of my first few encounters with him. I was young in my career. He cornered me in the coatroom at one of our holiday parties, grabbed my arm, and tried to kiss me. I yanked away from him and went back into the ballroom but said nothing. Not even to my then-husband for fear that he would probably have confronted him and caused me to lose my job. Sexual harassment was still unchartered water because the first national case was only two years prior. I saw how Anita Hill was treated when she accused Clarence Thomas of Sexual Harassment. I was not prepared to go through anything similar. A few months after the holiday party incident, this man tried to create a position for me on his team. I was called into a meeting with him but requested another person attend as a witness while I declined the position. After that, I avoided him because of his womanizing ways. Needless to say, even before the coatroom incident, I felt a spirit of lust on him.

For this, you know, that no fornicator, unclean person, nor covetous man, who is an idolater, has any inheritance in the kingdom of Christ and God. Ephesians 5:5. NKJV

The Know-It-All

The Know-It-All is the person who feels that they are the smartest in the class. Every time the teacher asks a question, they raise their hand, waving it around anxiously to let everyone else know they have the answer. This person challenges and attempts to out-wit everyone else. They are mental athletes, competitive in every aspect of the word. To say the least, these students are incredibly egotistical, obtaining and maintaining their position as the smartest in the class. If they ever provide the wrong answer, they get upset at anyone who competes with or laughs at them because knowledge is the essence of their identity.

In the workplace, the same behaviors are displayed, except the classroom is now the conference room. Instead of waving their hands to get attention, they just talk over people to make their points heard. This is the person in the workplace that you will find to be incredibly obnoxious. Despite their inability to give the floor to anyone else, you will have to admit that they know their stuff as they prepare for meetings and seem to have an answer for everything. You can say they are good at smooth-talking and making people believe they know what they are talking about. Most will not challenge this person because they are usually correct, becoming the subject matter expert (SME) on all subjects. Even if they are wrong, people will typically not catch the error because they don't question

Playground Personalities

this person's know-it-all ability.

I worked with a young woman who prided herself on being intelligent. People would constantly tell her how smart she was, and it went to her head. She became so prideful regarding her intelligence that she ridiculed people in roles she clearly was not qualified for. She was disrespectful of authority and only had loyalty to those who would help her move forward in her career. Her personality was a turn-off to most, but she was viewed as a subject matter expert because she aligned herself with department heads, imitated their behaviors, and mimicked their verbiage.

The icky side of her came out when she was threatened by someone who knew more than she did or was more qualified than she was. That unpleasant side was demonstrated by rebelliousness, outbursts of disrespectful statements, attempting to sabotage other employees. She was climbing the ladder of success and making many enemies along the way. At present, I believe she is enjoying the fruits of her labor. Still, one day she will look back and hopefully be embarrassed by her actions and repent of her behavior. If she does not, she will encounter people who will treat her like she has treated others.

> *But the wisdom that is from above is first pure, then peaceable, gentle, willing to yield, full of mercy and good fruits, without partiality and without hypocrisy.*

The Cast Of Characters

James 3:17 NKJV

The Lopsided Loyalist

The Lopsided Loyalist is a person that shows allegiance to a person or a group that absolutely has no love or respect for them.

They do everything in their power to defend the actions of the person or group of interest when everyone else can clearly see that they are being foolish. The group or person will either stab them in the back or blatantly treat them with disrespect, but the Lopsided Loyalist will remain committed, acting like their best friend.

I met a Lopsided Loyalist in a work setting. This phenomenal person was a Chief Executive Officer (CEO) who worked ridiculously hard and cared about the people she worked with. However, she was mild-mannered and did not rule with an iron fist. This made some people feel they were better equipped to be in her position, one person in particular, her Chief Financial Officer (CFO).

The CFO was a treacherous individual who gossiped about the CEO negatively and consistently. As a result, the CEO had several people resign due to their disdain, distrust, and discontentment with the CFO. Still, the CEO made excuses for her behavior and did nothing to satisfy the complaints.

Some complainers were good people who cared about the company but were not afforded grace for their mistakes. Instead, mistakes were magnified by the CFO in the form of attacks on their character, work ethic, and reputation. They were also, in some cases, people with years of knowledge and connections that would have benefited the organization.

While the CFO seemed to be winning by getting many people to quit, she was really losing because every action in the natural has a spiritual consequence. If she has not faced the consequences, she will at some point. I can respect the CFO's technical aptitude. She was good at Finance but terrible with people. I do not advocate keeping problem people or not giving corrective action. Their seniority, rank, or ability to perform the technical aspects of their job does not excuse harmful conduct. Everyone must be dealt with fairly and justly; their position title should not exempt them from the rules.

On the other hand, the CEO paid a hefty price for lopsided loyalty because she lost people that would support the culture and vision she was attempting to build. This made her road to success much harder than it had to be by being passive. She would have been better off replacing the CFO and keeping the masses who exited the organization.

A perverse man sows strife, and a whisperer separates the best of friends. Proverbs 16:28 NKJV

The Cast Of Characters

The Rumor-Mill Magician

The Rumor-Mill Magician is the real troublemaker of the bunch, although they seem to cause chaos and then worm their way out of it by making people believe someone else is the offender. They stir the pot amongst people by running from person to person, lying and gossiping to get some dirt or ammunition to tell another person. This character is similar to the Discord Cultivator, but the significant difference is that their intentions are blatantly hateful and malicious, with an end goal of seeing people fight or argue intensively. They make sure that their friends remain loyal to them while not liking one another.

In the office, the Rumor-Mill Magician goes from person to person, telling lies and embellishing truths. These people ruin the lives of others and cause their co-workers to lose their jobs and livelihoods. There is no remorse on behalf of the Rumor-Mill Magician because they feel that people deserve what they get or simply thrive on the chaos around them. These people's mouths are lethal weapons causing damage and mass destruction everywhere they go. Looking for people they can manipulate with their gossip and garbage.

I worked with a woman that used her mouth to ruin the lives of people she worked with. I remember one incident concerning her, where she used a co-worker's desk to answer the group phone lines. Unfortunately, the person forgot to lock her computer when she stepped away, and the Rumor-Mill Magician looked at her instant messages and learned that she was having an affair with a male co-worker.

The young woman was married to a gentleman that did not work in our organization but would hang out from time to time with people his wife worked with. The Rumor-Mill Magician took it upon herself to call the co-worker's husband to inform him of his wife's infidelity. This situation ignited conflict between the co-worker, her lover, and her husband. It also caused division within the group of co-workers that hung out with them. The Rumor-Mill Magician had no remorse and seemingly thrived on the conflict she had created. She stated that her co-worker deserved to be caught.

Although the affair situation was morally wrong, it was not the Rumor-Mill Magician's place to divulge that information. Similar to the Discord Cultivator, people were happy to see her go. The company's decision was to terminate her. A few years after she left, she had a very embarrassing situation that put her on the local news. People in the workplace talked about it and seemed pleased to hear of her downfall. I warned them that they should not rejoice in someone's pain despite their deeds.

For every kind of beast and bird, of reptile and creature of the sea, is tamed and has been tamed by mankind. But

> *no man can tame the tongue. It is an unruly evil, full of deadly poison. James 3:7-8 NKJV*

The Relevance Reacher

The Relevance Reacher is the one that goes out of their way to tell everyone how great they are, reaching out to anyone who will listen. In school, this person usually tells everyone how much their parents pay for their clothes and designer name brands. They talk themselves up and put everyone else down. In their minds and communications, no one is as good as them.

In the workplace, they tell you where they obtained their education and what degrees they have, how late they worked, how early they came in, or how many hours they worked on the weekend. This person is defined by their accomplishments, job, material possessions, looks, and perceived importance. If they have nothing to brag about pertaining to themselves, they will brag about their children, grandchildren, or anyone they can take credit for.

They wear their items of relevance like a badge of honor. In the workplace this person believes that hard work equates to 55 hours in the office weekly plus time on the weekend. They do not realize they are unbalanced because they are always trying to "one-up" or "out-do" the people around them. Their water-cooler conversations usually consist of

Playground Personalities

them finding a way to let you know what they have, how important their project is, how dedicated they are, or anything that makes them the topic of the conversation.

I have seen too many Relevance Reacher's in the workplace. So much so that I have difficulty picking one situation to write about. I will use a woman who constantly spoke of the size of the diamond her husband purchased for her and put people down whose engagement or wedding rings were more petite than she thought they should be. She talked about her expensive cars and home. She even detailed all the updates she was doing to her house. She would put other people down by letting them know she attended a Division One college and dismiss their education as irrelevant if they did not graduate from a similar university. This woman reached so far to be relevant that she started embezzling money from the company. She was purchasing expensive things, all the while stealing to support her lifestyle. The company Comptroller was a friend of hers from college, so she was incredibly quiet about the details of the incident, but I know that she had been accused of embezzling almost $60,000 from the company over one year. She was fired, but I do not know if she was prosecuted.

What would make a person go so far to impress others? Greed? Pride? Vanity? Insecurity? Fear? Envy? Who knows, maybe all of them, maybe some of them. Whatever the case, this person needs validation from outside sources because inside they are empty vessels.

Turn away my eyes from looking at worthless things and revive me in Your way. Psalm 119:37. NKJV

The Tattletale

There is a significant difference between someone who refuses to lie when confronted and someone who goes out of their way to tell what someone else has done. The characteristics of a Tattletale are that they look for and keep account of the things that someone does wrong to tell on them. Their only loyalty is to themselves. Please be assured, I am not condoning wrongdoing in any way, but I am speaking of the people that look for things for the sake of making other people look bad. My grandmother always said, "If you look for trouble, you will find it!" That means if you search for some drama, dirt, or wrongdoing, you will convince yourself of it. Sometimes you will be correct, but most of the time, you will be wrong. The Tattletale is usually the one that is doing all the dirt and would never tell what they are doing but live to tell what others are doing or have done.

In the classroom, this person is the one always threatening to tell the teacher about someone. Anything that someone does, they make the idle threat of informing the teacher.

Playground Personalities

The name for this person in the workplace is a mole. A mole is planted or identified with a plan to disclose information to upper management regarding their employees and how they really feel. These people are not brought in as consultants who will use feedback mechanisms to obtain the information ethically to better the culture. Instead, they are co-workers that show an allegiance to a manager or leader by betraying the confidence of their co-workers.

I worked with a woman who was driven by fear of losing a job due to her age. She was highly qualified for the role she held and really had a passion for her career, but her fear caused her to be treated disrespectfully by the office bully, who was also her boss. This person purchased gifts for special occasions and showed strong loyalty to the boss that she, on many occasions, stated she truly despised. Her peers questioned her integrity because her words did not match her actions. The sad thing about this situation is that the boss was not pleasant to her for a substantial portion of her tenure but only showed friendliness when she needed her to convey information about other co-workers. This woman sold her co-workers out and brought news to the manager about them in an attempt to gain favor.

Moreover, if your brother sins against you, go and tell him about his fault between you and him alone. If he hears you, you have gained your brother. But if he will not hear, take with you one or two more, that by the

> *mouth of the two or three witnesses every word may be established. Matthew 18:15-16. NKJV*

The Teacher's Pet

The infamous Teacher's Pet is met by everyone who has attended school. They are the ones that bring gifts to the teacher. They go out of their way to be the teacher's helper by volunteering to pass out papers, stay after school for projects and clean up after activities. They are usually the favored ones because their conduct demonstrates appreciation and loyalty toward the teacher. However, this person can be truly annoying! They are sugary-sweet to the teacher and often bitter and competitive with their fellow students. This makes them the object of disdain because their behaviors change when the teacher is present.

Does this sound like anyone you know in the workplace? They went from the teacher's pet to the (I hate this term) Brown-noser in the workplace. The definition of a Brown-noser as defined in the Collins Dictionary is: *"A person that agrees with someone important in order to get support. The activity of shamelessly seeking favor with someone."*

"I have met plenty of brown-noser's in my career, and I am sure you have met some in your organizations as well. However, one stands out in my mind, and here is what I remember about her.

Playground Personalities

She was close to and trusted by the boss. She pretended to be friends with some of her co-workers and would use any information she obtained against them by telling the boss all that she knew. She loved that there was disagreement between the boss and her co-workers because it kept her in a favorable position. The co-workers that saw through her antics avoided her. She was no longer able to pretend to be their friend because they did not trust her. She then displayed a nasty disposition toward those co-workers because she had to play a different game with them at that point. That game was finding fault in their work so that she could have something to use against them. She was a hard worker who knew her craft, and her manager felt she was invaluable because of all the problems and errors she found. This saved the manager time and effort because the Teacher's Pet was doing the work for her. However, it did not negate the problems, discord, and turnover that she caused within the team.

Why on earth could the manager not see that her "favorite" was the common factor in all the problems? If the manager calculated the amount of time and money it took to recruit, train, deal with employee complaints, and ultimately replace them, she would see that her blinders cost this company a pretty penny.

For do I now persuade men, or God? Or do I seek to please men? For if I still pleased men, I would not be a bondservant of Christ. Galatians 1:10 NKJV

The Cast Of Characters

The Temper-Tot

The temperamental child grows up to be the "overly passionate adult." I really get tired of people misbehaving, throwing temper tantrums, and using the word "passionate." I mean, come on, I know passion means you will put your heart and soul into something you believe in, but it does not provide an excuse to misbehave. I am sure you have encountered the child whose parents could not control them, and they acted out in public so that they could get their way. Although embarrassed, the parents were hostage to their child's demands. These out-of-control children grow up and enter our organizations with their "overly passionate" personalities. People walk on eggshells to keep from setting off the land mines of their challenging dispositions. They have frequent blow-ups, depending on their mood at the moment, and because most people avoid conflict like the plague, they just avoid this person or go above and beyond to keep from igniting one of their many trigger points.

I had a boss that literally scared most people, and he reveled in the fact that people feared him because he equated it with respect. It did not take much to set him off, and before you knew it, he was yelling, red in the face, biting his lip, or rubbing his forehead, seemingly to keep from hitting someone. He would never apologize for his behavior and often say things like, "I am passionate about it." His behavior was childish and annoying. But because he was the boss, most people would not challenge him.

He would drop the "F-bomb" in the presence of all of his staff members. He had an unbelievably lousy temper, and a low tolerance for anyone who stood up for the rules, challenged him or did not stroke his enormous ego. He would call people names like an idiot and seemed to wait on the opportunity to embarrass them in meetings where he felt most powerful, in the presence of other people who feared him. Unfortunately, he has ruined many lives and yet continues to hold his position. His behavior and affairs continue because no one he respects will draw a line in the sand and tell him how detestable his behavior is. The organization is suffering, its reputation in that city is terrible, and its turnover rate is enormous.

A quick-tempered man acts foolishly, and a man of wicked intentions is hated. Proverbs 14:17. NKJV

The Two-Faced

The Two-Faced is the person who does whatever it takes to please the person they are in front of at the time. They like you as long as there is no one around to impress. As soon as they are around the wrong influences, they will disrespect you, pick on or taunt you. These children are confusing because just when things appear to be good, they will show the other side of their face, which is ugly. Jekyll and Hyde! Two completely different personalities in one person.

This behavior continued into adulthood, and this child became the "Back-Stabber." I have seen many of those who engaged in conversations about a person and make others believe they did not care for that person. However, in the presence of that person their story and actions change. These people are dangerous. Remember, if they talk about someone else to you, they will talk about you to them.

I recall a situation where I worked on a project team with two of my peers. One of the peers felt that they were doing work that was beneath them and conveyed that frequently. This person automatically made himself the leader of this small project team and started speaking condescendingly to the other member of the team and me. I had no problem standing up for myself, but one day I had to address his behavior toward her too. He went to higher-ups, stated that we were the problem children, and blamed us for delays on the project. All the delays were due to his disagreements, but he did not tell them that part. I would literally listen to her scream and yell after calls with this guy. She spoke clearly about how she really despised him and felt he was arrogant. When the time came for us to discuss the problems in the presence of our bosses, she acted as though she was unaware of any problems on the project team. She shrugged her shoulders, looked at him, and pointed to me. She pretended like that was the first time she heard the problems and did not express any concern about him. I spoke honestly and openly to resolve the problems. My story did not change in his presence or our bosses. After the meeting, she came to me apologizing and attempted to talk about his behavior during the meeting. I looked at her and told her I was disappointed in her coward-like behavior, and she could no longer discuss any problems with me.

For it is not an enemy who reproaches me; then I could bear it. Nor is it one who hates me who has exalted himself against me; then I could hide from him. But it was you, a man my equal, my companion and acquaintance.
Psalm 55: 12-13 NKJV

The Vicious Viper

The Vicious Viper is usually seen as hateful or all-out evil by most people. They are downright cruel in every essence of the word. They seem to enjoy finding ways to embarrass people by using social media to lash out or plan schemes to see their demise. Cruelty is their fuel. The unfortunate thing is that sometimes, they are popular and lead a group of minions that are vicious too. In school, this person usually has influence over people because of popularity and the social limelight. This person grows up and enters the workforce with the same cruel, self-indulged attitude that has been tolerated or rewarded for so long that it is ingrained in their personality. Just like a viper, they strike with no regret, concern, or feeling.

I observed a Payroll Manager who was a Vicious Viper. Why someone put this person in a position to deal with internal customers is beyond my understanding, but she had the position and took no prisoners. She knew she had the power to mess up payroll checks, deny pay advances, or delay paychecks. She had complaints lodged because she cursed at employees, flipped them off, and made it difficult to get anything done through her. Everyone complained about this hateful individual, but the Company did nothing and retained her without any repercussions. She was thorough, detail-oriented, and good at the technical aspects of her job as well. Unfortunately, this discourteous soul lacked empathy and blatantly used her power to make people suffer.

I recall an incident where an employee had their moving van stolen during their move. They had no money or household items and needed the Company to cut a check for their accrued vacation time to purchase some emergency items while the police attempted to recover her things. This Payroll Manager refused to help the employee in need. This is just one of several examples of her unwillingness to help a person in need.

The people who she liked possessed similar characteristics of hatefulness. They were able to get along well because they were cut from the same cloth. Even her boss said she had a nasty personality but did nothing about it. If this organization were sticklers about accountability and integrity, they would have held her accountable a long time ago as opposed to overlooking her behavior and saying, "That's just how she is!"

One day she will have a need for someone to do something to help her. I hope she will have humbled herself and repented before that time comes. Otherwise, she will reap what she has sown and understand what it was like for those employees she mistreated.

Therefore, lay aside all filthiness and overflow of wickedness, and receive with meekness the implanted word, which can save your souls. James 1:21 NKJV

The Want-To-Be

The childhood Want-To-Be is the person who does not have an original thought in their own head regarding how to think, act or dress. This person finds their identity in the people they hang out with. They dress the way that the "in-crowd" dresses and behave in the same manner. Often times they bring those behaviors home and show feelings of displaced anger. These children act out because they are seeking identity and validation. Why? Because they are not able to validate themselves.

The Cast Of Characters

In the workplace, they are the same. You will find them imitating and mimicking the style of someone they admire. They are like chameleons because they have learned to mimic and fit in by changing their true colors to match their environment. Rarely will you get to know the true essence of this person because they do not know themselves. As a result, they lose themselves in character, mimicking others. They lose respect along the way.

I once worked with a lady who indeed was a lovely person from the onset. Her problem was that she was overly ambitious and started hanging out with a young woman who had an intense sense of entitlement and an assertive attitude to go along with it. The lovely young lady seemed to immediately adopt the negative behaviors of this less than desirable person until there appeared to be no more traits of niceness in her. She went from a respectable person to an arrogant ugly-acting individual for the sake of climbing the corporate ladder. She became so much like the person she was emulating that you really could not tell them apart by their actions.

Do not be misled: Bad company corrupts good character.
1 Corinthians 15:33 NIV

The Warrior

The Warrior is the person that fights every battle. They are viewed as aggressive people because they will stand up to anyone. At times this is a good thing if used in its proper context or position. However, a warrior without wisdom is dangerous. For instance, if someone is a Union Steward and is advocating for the rights of the person who has voiced a grievance or if they see injustice and raise their concerns with diplomacy, it is a good thing. It is not so good when it is just that person's way of communicating. Meaning, they make everything an argument because they need to be right or feel a need to interject their opinion without using wisdom. The Warrior may be great on a debate team in school, but they are contentious in the workplace. They have their thoughts and views in school and do not hang in a clique, although they can usually blend and not stand out. They will stand up for everything they feel is an injustice.

I worked in a place where lack of rules and entitlement seemed to be the norm. The entire senior management team had changed. The staff was traumatized by the previous leader, who ruled with an iron fist. The new leader had some great ideas but seemed to go out of her way to appease people opposed to holding them accountable. She would often say, "They will either get on board with the new culture or leave." Although this was true in some cases, the damage the people did while in the organization or after they left was exorbitant. This particular CEO was too passive, and this caused infighting amongst the Executive Team. In this organization, the Warrior that manifested was a woman I could see from the start was an anointed child of God. A few weeks after she started, I asked her how she was adapting to the work environment, and she told me it was difficult. The word she used to describe it was Babylon. I could relate to what she was feeling due to the chaos in that environment. I followed the guidance of the Holy Spirit and advised her to stay prayerful and in God's will because her assignment was more significant than just the work she had been hired to do.

The organization was shifting from a Christian-based agency to having no Christian values at all. With all the changes, came agendas that seemed to take precedence over more important things. The important things were clients' safety, employee relations, financial outcomes, and federal compliance. Because the Warrior was not prayed up daily, she was attacked constantly from the spiritual disturbances she felt in her environment. She would confront managers in meetings by opposing agendas focused on LGBTQ and the acceptance of other religions. As you would imagine, her objections were not received well because many of the staff members and clients were not Christians. Although she was not wrong in her opinions about keeping other orders of business a priority that focused on client safety and compliance, she failed to use wisdom in how she presented her views. It seemed like an attack to the managers who embraced LGBTQ lifestyles or practiced other religions. She also was unable to analyze the organization's culture shift and desire to embrace everything except Christianity. She ended up making a human mistake that caused her to leave the organization. After she left, she was gossiped about and made to be a terrible person, which was not true. In that case, I was happy for her to go because I knew she was a Warrior who lacked wisdom. She failed to control what came out of her mouth, and that was not good for her. I pray that as she grows in knowledge and self-discipline, she will be able to handle the assignments given to her by God.

You will not need to fight in this battle. Position yourselves, stand still and see the salvation of the Lord, who is with you, O Judah, and Jerusalem! Do not fear or be dismayed; tomorrow go out against them, for the Lord is with you. 2 Chronicles 20:17. NKJV

The Whining Brat

The Whining Brat is the person that constantly complains about everything. They find a problem for every proposed solution. For them, the glass is always half empty. They usually blame everyone else for them not getting ahead or causing the issues in their life. They look outward, not inward. Whenever someone else is being promoted or recognized, they will find something negative about them and focus on that. This person has difficulty functioning in a world that does not see them through rose-colored glasses, although they fail to see others in a positive light.

The Cast Of Characters

A fitting example of the Whining Brat is a Rock & Roll Icon from the forties and fifties who I refuse to name. However, I found him highly entertaining because, in every interview, he exercised the opportunity to say that he created Rock & Roll and that everyone stole from him. It seemed like a desperate attempt to get, what he felt, was his deserved recognition. Whatever the case, he was genuinely a Whining Brat.

An example of this I faced in an organization was a guy I hired to help with a project in recruitment. He had an agenda to be hired on permanently and take over my job as Director. One he clearly was not qualified for. But, on the other hand, he was a good talker, so he made people believe he was capable and dedicated.

When he got into the project, he did not get the candidates through the process. His teammates had to carry him and pick up the slack. On the day of this large recruitment fair, the HR Directors from other cities that came to assist talked about how unorganized he was, and it was clear to them that he was the weakest link on my team. When I brought the concerns forward, this man attacked his teammates and me. He stated he was more qualified than them, brought in more talent, and said I was not a good leader. He whined, lied, and did everything he could to not accept any responsibility for his lack of dedication and lousy performance.

Do all things without complaining and disputing that you may become blameless and harmless, children of God without fault in the midst of a crooked and perverse generation, among whom you shine as lights in the world, holding fast the word of life, so that I may rejoice in the day of Christ that I have not run in vain or labored in vain.
Philippians 2:14-16. NKJV

The Wimp

The Wimp is the person that is either too nice, too shy, or too passive. This is the child that is often the target of the bully because they are easy to manipulate. They try not to draw attention to themselves because some form of fear drives them. Their fear could be arguing, fighting, gaining negative attention, losing respect from an authority figure, or facing ridicule. Whatever the fear is, it seemingly drives their actions and makes them unable to stand up for themselves.

In the workplace, this person is the "Push-Over." They do not display a backbone of any kind in dealing with their co-workers, managers, or subordinates. This person often loses respect because they do not stand for anything. This person will usually turn a blind eye to avoid rocking a boat or standing up to someone with a more assertive personality.

I worked with a manager who had no control over his team. He was such a passive man, and his team took complete advantage of him. Attendance, low productivity, and team conflicts were the results of his lack of assertiveness. After a while, he was removed from management, and his team was dispersed to other managers. These team members struggled with being held accountable and many of them ended up leaving the organization because they could not cope. They had become so accustomed to not being led or held liable that when they were, they complained.

It was clear that the Wimp of a manager was not good for them, and his passivity was not fit for leadership. He was a nice man but not a good manager.

So, whoever knows the right thing to do and fails to do it, for him it is sin. James 4:17 ESV

The Witch

I do not believe in good and evil witches. Their power comes from darkness; therefore, a witch is a witch. Some of them have more wicked intentions, polluted hearts, and seared consciousness than others and that will depict what they do with the power they conjure. They exist among us and are in the workplace. If someone is using witchcraft to gain favor or to curse someone, they are outside the will of God. I have encountered witches and warlocks in workforces that did not mind identifying themselves as such.

Playground Personalities

I do not know how or why these people got involved in these things. Were these practices passed down through family bloodlines? Did they have bad experiences that made them bitter, leading to seeking help from the dark side? Were they wanting fortune and fame and willing to sell their soul to get it? Who knows, but they are real and living amongst us. If you need confirmation go to the app called TikTok or even YouTube. They do not hide their identity and take pride in being rebellious to God.

I worked with a guy who asked me on two occasions what I was reading during my lunch period. The first time I told him the title of the book was "The Game of Life and How to Play It" by Florence Scovel Shinn. He seemed to engage asking what the book was about. The second time he asked, which was a couple of weeks later, I told him I was reading the "Bondage Breaker" by Neil T. Anderson. He looked at me with an expression of disgust. He came into my office a few hours later and told me that I needed to denounce my faith and join forces with them. He stated that he knew masonic handshakes, symbols, and different things but didn't know how or where he obtained the knowledge. He stated that the world needs to have one money currency and said he knew how to astral project. I had not heard of anything called astral projecting and did not clearly understand everything he was speaking of, but I knew it was not good. I also knew I wanted him far away from me.

The Cast Of Characters

I asked him if he was stating that he was the Anti-Christ. He said that he was not the Anti-Christ, but he was in the belly of Satan. I calmly told him I would never denounce my faith and wished him a good evening. He left my office, and my assistant came in and asked if she heard the conversation correctly, and I told her, "Yes and that was weird!" I left work about an hour later and took the train home. I lived about 40 minutes away from the job. When I got home, I turned on the light in my bedroom and he was lying on my bed. He quickly disappeared, and I began to pray, anoint my home and my bed until I felt the presence go away. I prayed at other times because I smelled foul smells on my bed that reminded me of rotten eggs. I would pray and the smell would leave. I knew it was connected to him. I avoided him after that but stayed in prayer about him. I had observed other things he did, but this was enough to make you understand the level of the Warlock I had encountered.

On another occasion, I had a manager come to me about an attendance record of an employee that she needed to do a formal written warning. When she showed me the attendance record, the employee should have been counseled months prior. I asked the manager why this employee had not been issued corrective action like others in the past, and the manager seemed reluctant to tell me. I worked with this manager for years and knew she was always on top of these matters, so I pushed her to talk to me. She told me that the employee was known for making Voodoo dolls of people who crossed her. I met with the employee and her manager and informed her that she was due for corrective action due to attendance violations.

As I spoke to the employee, she started chanting something while I was speaking. I did not know what she was saying, so after she chanted, I rebuked and prayed. I went to church that same week and was called up for prayer by the prophet. I was told that the place I work in is very demonic and that I had encountered a witch who tried to speak a curse of death over me. She prayed over me and told me to stay consecrated. After that, I did not come back in contact with that employee again.

But the cowardly, unbelieving, abominable, murderers, sexually immoral, sorcerers, idolaters, and all liars shall have their part in the lake which burns with fire and brimstone, which is the second death.
Revelation 21:8. NKJV

I am sure you have seen some of these characters in your workplaces, churches, and schools. As stated before, our battle is not with people but the spiritual forces influencing them. Failure to get our flesh under submission will result in consequences of bad behavior. Behavior that will damage our growth, our reputations, our relationships, and ultimately our destiny.

Now the works of the flesh are evident, which are adultery, fornication, uncleanness, lewdness, idolatry, sorcery, hatred, contentions, jealousies, outbursts of wrath, selfish ambitions, dissensions, heresies, envy, murders, drunkenness, revelries, and the like; of which I tell you beforehand, just as I also told you in time past, that those who practice such things will not inherit the kingdom of God. But the manifestation of the Spirit is love, joy, peace, longsuffering, kindness, goodness, faithfulness, gentleness, self-control. Against such there is no law. And those who are Christ's have crucified the flesh with its passions and desires. If we live in the Spirit, let us also walk in the Spirit. Let us not become conceited, provoking one another, envying one another. Galatians 5:19-26. NKJV

Time to Reflect

- Have you observed any of these personalities in your workplace? Which ones? How did they affect you?

- Were you able to recognize the seven deadly sins in most of these situations?

- Have you personally had an experience with someone you knew was tampering with powers of darkness? How did you handle it? How would you handle it now?

- Which of these examples are Explorers, Settlers, or

Playground Personalities

Followers?

- Do you see similarities to the children you encountered in school?

Chapter 6

All Organizations Speak. What Does Yours Say?

You will find that all the characters fall into a category of an Explorer, Settler, or Follower, as mentioned in chapter two. In observing these characters in the boardrooms, cubicles, offices, and meeting rooms of non-profit organizations, Fortune 100, and Fortune 500 companies, I wondered how on earth these people were allowed to keep their jobs! I also wondered why none of my college classes prepared me to deal with the drama and craziness of people in the workplace. Working hard, being dependable, knowledgeable, and treating others with respect is not the secret to longevity in the workplace. The key to longevity seems to be managing politics, overlooking some terrible behaviors, swallowing your dignity, ignoring wrongdoing, refusing to rock the boat, and basically maneuver the landmines of the difficult personalities.

Playground Personalities

Company policies, values, behaviors, and ethical commitments are put in place to state what the workplace culture is ideally supposed to be. Still, the true determinant of culture is the TOLERATED BEHAVIOR of the employees, especially those in management roles.

I do not know how many times I have been dismayed by corporate branding paraphernalia. It will state collaboration, accountability, integrity, respect, innovation, leadership, and authenticity as their values because it sounds good. I believe it is an attempt to disillusion themselves into thinking they demonstrate this conduct. Yet, there is NO evidence of these values in most organizations.

With the lack of congruency between the written statements and tolerated behaviors of staff members, I started journaling about organizational cultures around 1998 to answer some of the questions I had, such as:

- Why were some dynamic and fast-paced?
- Why were some stagnant and slow-moving?
- Why were some like a close familial community?
- Why were some unorganized and discombobulated?
- Why did sub-cultures seem to exist from department to department?
- Why did some of them attract young people?
- Why were some full of older workers with

high tenure?
- Why are some unable to retain good employees?

I have been fortunate to experience and observe strong cultures and others that were being transformed. Those strong cultures had key people who fought hard to maintain that status quo. If activities and exercises were conducted to identify problems or prove if the culture was connected to the vision, there was resistance. The middle and senior managers did not want to participate in activities that caused them to be evaluated by their peers and employees to address their own weaknesses. In fact, most felt that because they had obtained these positions, there was no room for them to grow. They were legends in their own minds, whose egos and pride kept them from accepting feedback from their peers and subordinates.

The only way to resolve a problem is to first acknowledge it. America, as a whole, has a culture of facing symptoms of issues and therefore not addressing the root causes. I believe this is why racism, classism, sexism, and religious discrimination continue to be at the forefront of about every social and political issue in this country. We make a little progress and sweep the remainder of the mass issue under the carpet until it eventually bubbles up in the form of civil unrest, where we are forced to address it again. If the media stops covering it, we are so busy living our lives and distracted by reality TV and entertainment that we forget about the problems. We just do not have the tenacity needed to dig deep and resolve issues, so we just address the symptoms hoping the rest of the problem will magically disappear.

The impact of tenure on culture

The average tenure of employees seems to be connected to the organization's culture. High-tenured organizations and cultures have employees that stay past five years. The attributes of these corporations are:

- Slower-paced work environment
- Antiquated systems
- If it ain't broke, don't fix it mentality. "We've always done it that way."
- You are still considered new until you have been with them for about five years.
- Promotions are based on seniority, not knowledge or skills to move to the next level.
- Pay increases are based on seniority scales.
- Extreme loyalty to the organization.
- Bad attitudes toward people who do not have their company-based knowledge.
- An entitlement mentality.
- Lots of unspoken "common knowledge" rules that are not written.
- Lots of first- and second-year turnover because

newcomers do not feel welcome or appreciated in this culture.
- Resistant to change.

Examples of high tenured organizations are government and union jobs. Unions have played an integral role in forming standards and better working conditions in the years where there were no laws or government entities to oversee problems relating to workplace safety, discrimination, and fair pay. However, in our society today, I believe that unions sometimes (depending on the union) create bureaucracy, stifle teamwork, and inhibit a corporation from rewarding its star performers. In addition, they keep great employees in positions they cannot advance in by brainwashing them into thinking that jobs outside the union are bad. Finally, and most of all, unions prevent the organizations from making necessary changes to evolve without negotiating matters and decisions that management should be able to make to keep the organization from becoming vulnerable financially and possibly becoming extinct.

Low tenured employee culture is where most employee's turnover within the first three years. The attributes of these corporations are:
- Faster paced work environment.
- No loyalty to the employer. "What's in it for me"

- mentality.
- High turnover.
- Unqualified people in high-ranking roles because they have managed to outlive the people that started with them.
- Lots of discombobulation because by the time someone becomes a subject matter expert (SME), they are out of the door.
- Comfortable with change.
- Inconsistency in getting things done. Lots of errors and repeating things that have already been done.
- Low productivity.

Companies need a mix of high and low tenure to avoid the disadvantages of being on extreme ends of the pendulum. High-tenured employees bring a wealth of historical knowledge that can keep an organization from making huge mistakes and setting new precedents that may not work. Low-tenured employees bring the value of innovative ideas and experiences from other organizations that can keep an organization innovative and relevant. With these combined, you get the tenure in the middle of the scale where it needs to be and have a chance of forming a culture that is innovative as opposed to stagnant.

Workplace Games and Politics

There are many games played in corporations, hence the

name of the book. The games I have observed the most are:

- The "Longest Hours in a Workday" game. The game rules are to come to work early or stay late hours, then brag about how many hours you spend at work.

- The "Prove You Work Unorthodox Hours" game. The game rules are to send emails on weekends or in the wee hours of the morning so that there is a timestamp proving you are ever so committed to your jobs.

- The "Master Delegator" game. Rules are to never really do the work but constantly take on new projects or tasks and then piggyback or delegate the majority of the work to others. Then, if the end result is positive, take credit for it, but throw someone under the bus if the result is negative.

- The "Social Decision Maker's" game. Rules are to socialize with co-workers frequently outside of work, build camaraderie, make important decisions at the golf course or the bar, then come back to work and make everyone else live with the decisions made by like-minded people.

- The "No Accountability" game. Rules are to refuse to hold people accountable and to set no boundaries to govern their behavior. So, when you see someone misbehaving, say, "Oh, that's just how they are!" and

Playground Personalities

expect everyone else to be okay with it.

- The "Hire Diverse Candidate" game. The rules are to make a concerted effort to find and hire the female in a male-dominated role or the person of color into the dominant Caucasian team, but purposely make them uncomfortable and feel ostracized by the group. Then, when the person resigns, just say, "We tried, but they weren't a fit!"

- The "Personal Life Competition" game. Rules are to use material items to show that you are affluent, disregard educational degrees if they did not come from a particular school, openly brag about where you live if it is in a prestigious area, describe your children as perfect humans who have never made a mistake, and remember to crush others who do not have what you have.

- The "Sink or Swim in the Silent Rule Pool" game. The rules are to watch the newly hired team member try to figure out the expectations of their job, purposely avoid providing them with the knowledge to make their job easy, shun them so that they are left to speculate why they are being mistreated until they are so uncomfortable that they leave the organization.

- The "No One Can Do It Better Than Me" game. The rules are to provide the minimum amount of information so that the new person will get frustrated, inundated, and make mistakes. But, of course, this makes the new person look bad while keeping the trainer in a position as the subject matter expert, thereby keeping the power.

Cynical, I know, but oh so true! One of the hardest things in the world is to see the wrongdoing, shortcomings, or involvement in these things as part of an organizations or department's culture.

Systemic Ignorance

Systemic Ignorance is where the organization chooses to disregard the internal problems, even when they are made aware of them. They cover up or just dismiss the concerns because either they do not care, are too arrogant to believe they will ever get caught or have accepted the culture as it is. The managers do not understand they can be named personally in a civil suit and do not possess ownership of mitigating risk to the company they work for.

Another form of systemic ignorance is when the company practices do not mirror the written mission, vision, and values statements. This is when the company says things like:

— We have a liberal work/life balance policy, but the practice of the management team is to frown upon anyone that takes their allotted PTO, wants to telecommute, or needs to have a flexible work schedule.

- We are an equal opportunity employer, but the hiring practices are discriminatory. An example is having credit checks for jobs that do not have a bona fide occupational need for credit. You can also look at the representatives of the organization and see that there is no equal employment.

- We promote from within, but the management team is typically hired from the outside.

- We value diversity, but the company does not make reasonable accommodations to meet the needs of a diverse workforce. An example would be accommodating a religious holiday.

- We have a philosophy to coach for success, but the employees only receive disciplinary action or negative feedback from their managers opposed to balanced feedback that provides their strengths as well.

Human Resources (HR) Does Not Mean Hide and Rescue

One of the many reasons I joined the HR profession was the perceived integrity that embodied the field and how

All Organizations Speak. What Does Yours Say?

HR affects every area of an organization. Unfortunately, I believe HR is one of the most underappreciated disciplines. A discipline that should be respected for the required knowledge, such as conflict resolution skills, detailed records and documentation, compliance with federal, state, and local laws, training, and development skills, and ensuring ethics and values are at the forefront of everything the company stands for. It is so difficult to understand why there is usually a battle between operations managers and Human Resources. Not partnering with HR is like biting the hand that feeds you. Most operations managers do not value any department that is not generating profit. Still, they do not look at the money they are saving with the services HR provides, like reduced turnover, mitigating risks of lawsuits, and possible work stoppages.

Human Resources (HR) is the department that is supposed to ensure that the risks to the company are limited by implementing policies and procedures for administering the guidelines. Most importantly, management demonstrates or models the appropriate behaviors, values, and ethics, not by policing but by hiring the right people, training, and coaching them. This means that HR's loyalty is to the company (the entity). The unfortunate thing is that because most HR personnel receive their paycheck from the very bosses that they are supposed to be keeping honest, so many have sold their soul by using their knowledge to cover up wrongdoing and executing the agendas of senior management, showing loyalty to the people, not the entity. HR does not mean Hide the problems & Rescue the people from their consequences!

This lack of integrity has caused many employees to not trust HR because they have seen their loyalty to upper management and have witnessed them not doing the right thing for the organization by being fair and honest. As a result, HR in many organizations is viewed as a dirty cop. The cop that took an oath to serve and protect but instead decided to take a bribe and line their pockets with hush money. I have spent many days trying to win employees' trust at all levels because of previous experiences with HR personnel. In some cases, I have been successful, but in others, I have failed miserably. I failed because the systemic ignorance was so engraved in the fabric of the culture that only divine power could make the necessary changes.

Whistleblowers

A whistleblower is a person that informs the public or those in positions of authority of wrongdoing. I personally believe that whistleblowers are necessary for some organizations because exposure brings resolution to problems. However, in most cases, whistleblowers are seen as troublemakers because they do not fall into the "Stepford Wife" way of behaving in an organization. The Stepford Wives is a movie directed by Bryan Forbes that was introduced in 1975. It is about a suburban community where all the wives are docile and subservient. This community was created by men who wanted these types of wives. When a couple would move into the neighborhood, the women would be converted one by one. A rebellious wife moved into the neighborhood and discovered that the husbands in the community were making robots of their wives. While there are no physical robots in organizations, there are most undoubtedly mental robots; people come into the organization and adapt to the culture's norms and values and negate their own. While there is nothing wrong with order and decency, there is something wrong when people come into an organization and conform to negative values and behaviors.

I define a whistleblower as someone who sees wrongdoing and does not ignore it. They dare to report the problems instead of condoning them by doing nothing. Whistleblowers, in most cases, have integrity. Please do not confuse a whistleblower with someone who really does go from organization to organization looking for problems to report, that is a troublemaker. Instead, I refer to those who allow their moral compass to lead them by exposing things they know are wrong, unethical, or unsafe. They understand they may have a cost to pay by taking the stand, and this cost could be ostracization, losing their job, or being retaliated against. In the light of their circumstances, they rise to the occasion by standing on integrity even if they are standing alone. I commend these people!

Leadership

I often ask myself; how do we have tons of books on leadership basics; yet we overlook it when our so-called leaders are acting up? Managers are almost always held to a lower standard than the employees they lead. Still, we are quick to hold line-level employees accountable for their wrongdoing and allow managers to do whatever they want. This wrong message permeates throughout the organization and creates a division between management and their staff.

We all know that authentic leadership is not defined by a person's title or position, right? So why are we okay with referring to a "manager" synonymously with a "leader"? I found many definitions that basically stated a leader is someone with a management title. That is not always the case. A leader can bring out the best in people who feel grateful to be a part of what that leader stands for. A true leader may not be in a position of management at all. It could be the janitor you walk past every day who takes great pride in cleanliness. The receptionist who greets people and represents the company with enthusiasm. The administrative assistant who works hard to ensure their boss has everything they need to focus on high-level tasks. Leaders have a great deal of integrity, wisdom, vision, and care for human beings.

I have seen people in very high-level positions who were not leaders at all. Being a leader comes with great responsibility to guide, protect, and correct the people they lead. A leader realizes that God has put them in place to help the people see what responsibility and true Christianity looks like. When I think of the ministry Jesus had on earth, I noticed he was rarely in the churches and synagogues. He was humble, loving, willing to teach with boldness and honesty, did not look down on people, focused on God's business and divine purpose, mentored people, took time to help and support people, showed compassion for human weakness, and demonstrated God's actual expectations of us. Jesus came against religious spirits that kept people in bondage and prevented them from genuinely believing God loved them. Religious people hated Jesus, who did not believe who he was, went out of their way to prove him wrong, attack his character, and ultimately crucify him. But they did not realize that they were being used to fulfill prophecy and birth Christianity.

Ethics Lines

Do not fool yourself into believing that when you contact an ethics hotline, you are guaranteed confidentiality. Ethics hotlines are only as effective as the measures put in place to ensure confidentiality. If the ethics line is a third-party, it is better than a company-managed ethics line. Company-managed ethics lines are only as ethical as the people who manage the hotline, their influence in the culture, and the culture's attitude toward complainers. Suppose the organizational culture is not supportive of accountability and keeping the culture ethical. In that case, the person managing the line will be ineffective because of the people involved in the complaint, unethical in their own regard, or ineffective because they have no power to do the right thing.

The success of ethics lines is dependent on senior management and organizational culture. I have managed Ethics lines and find that if the senior managers or legal department did not take the recommendations given or truly stand for ethical behavior, they would sweep the problem under the rug or pat the bad guy on the hand.

I have also seen ethics lines managed by outside vendors so that people could speak openly and honestly. When the complaints were sent to the unethical organization, the managers would discuss the matter, figuring out who the complaining party was. The whistleblowers were viewed as the bad guys for reporting the issue. In most cases, the whistleblower left the company, their position was eliminated, or they would stack the evidence against them until they felt good about terminating them.

On the flip side, I have witnessed people using ethics lines for personal reasons also. They reported complaints that should have been handled by their management or Human Resources department. In these cases, the problems were not ethical issues but revealed concerns with management or the organizational culture. As a result, the reports were received, and management was provided training to handle problems, or the organization recognized the need for change and worked to improve the culture.

Time to Reflect

- What Corporate games have you witnessed?

- What things in your organization seem to go against what they say they stand for?

- How are people treated who bring issues to management?

Chapter 7

Can I Be Honest?

Most organizations, especially those with high turnover rates, have many reasons people leave their toxic work environments. Still, most do not realize it is because of them and the cultures they have created. If companies would just be honest, this is what an offer letter would look like:

Dear Dreamer,

On behalf of myself and my esteemed colleagues, we would like to congratulate you on accepting the position of <u>Disillusioned Professional</u>. We are so excited about you joining our team and cannot wait to sap your energy, prove to you that you are not that special and genuinely make you question why you came here.

You will begin your position on May 15, 2021, reporting to the <u>Vice President of Employee Disengagement</u>. Your *annual salary will be $85,000, but because we do not want to invest the correct amount in benefits, you will only receive about 2/3 of that, which you will not enjoy because you will be required to be in the office for at least 55 hours per week. You will be eligible to receive 2 weeks of paid vacation, but we expect you to work through it, hence the reason we call it paid. We have a pricy medical, dental, and vision plan that you will surely take advantage of because your mental state, diet, and vision will diminish quickly with the long hours, inability to prepare healthy meals, and anxiety created by the environment. Our prescription plan is also very reasonable because you will undoubtedly be using weight loss supplements, anti-anxiety pills, and possibly Rogaine or Keranique to regrow the hair you will lose from stress.*

We are so happy you chose to join our dysfunctional team. We cannot wait to see how long it will take to prove you are the disillusioned professional we hired you to be and to see you become cynical, bitter, and disengaged like the rest of us. Please be advised that no training, assistance, or any form of support will be provided to you as this is a sink or swim environment. We will test your knowledge, challenge your will, and sabotage you every chance we get. When we are done with you, the only choice you will have is to become one of us or to leave. Of course, we hope that you will go to make room for the next victim.

Please be advised, we are an "At Will" Employer. This means, if you expect us to live the values that we post or complain in any manner about our dysfunctional culture, we will indeed find a way to get rid of you immediately along with the other disillusioned professionals that preceded you. Lastly, we will see to it that your reputation is destroyed so that you will wish you had not been a rebel and blew the whistle on our secrets.

Again, congratulations, and thank you for joining our dysfunctional team!

Sincerely,

The HR (Hide & Rescue) Department

I have had many senior managers who expected me to execute their agendas. They quickly learned that I would not, and I became their target for belittlement or termination. I have never been, nor will I ever be, the Hide & Rescue person. I can think of two scenarios where my opinion was not popular:

- I was once on an Executive Team of twelve people. I was the only person of color on this team. We were charged with having to make some immediate decisions about ways to save money. I offered to cut money on the current year's employee recognition program. They opposed that because they felt it would decrease morale. They offered to cut jobs as if that would not affect morale. I resisted that because I was more concerned about sustaining people's livelihood. Since I was outnumbered, I listened. It came down to the positions of three black managers. It was my job to keep the company honest and out of court and terminating three minorities would not send the right message unless there was a valid reason, a standard set of criteria. I asked what criteria we were using to choose these managers, only to find none. I said it needs to be based on either seniority, performance, or redundancy in job function. When we looked at those factors, those were not the managers that should have been cut. It came down to two Executive Assistants of our two top managers and another Black manager who was close friends with the second highest ranking manager. They would not hear of it, but it was the right thing to do. I would not support their recommendation, and it was not a popular opinion. The cost to me was this high-ranking second manager, who was known for being vindictive, took a committee away from me while I was out on a two-week medical leave. This committee was a community service team that was birth between myself and my previous boss, who had a heart for supporting the community. This committee did not have a budget, and we raised money to do the things we did in the community. At the end of the year, we had received accolades from the General Manager and Corporate Office, and this initiative was used as a requirement nationwide. I cried for a few days when I learned what he had done, but I should have expected it because I challenged him by offering his Executive Assistant and his friend's jobs to be cut based on criteria.

- I was on another small Executive team where there were two top leaders. I reported to the Vice President of Operations. She did not like the Director of Operations, who also reported to her. When we were in meetings, she would send nasty messages about the Director of Operations via Blackberry to me. I hated it and found it childish and disrespectful. This woman was cut-throat, and I recognized this from her behavior. I had to challenge this woman about a decision to cut the jobs of nine women, all over the age of 40, in a program she created and made many promises to them that she would do everything in her power to see them succeed. When she failed to keep her promise, I reminded her of that. She proceeded with the job cuts and took my recommendation to give them a severance package to avoid a lawsuit based on age discrimination. The nine women met with me privately to discuss the pros and cons of accepting the severance. I explained that they could be tied up in court for years trying to fight it and agreed that it was a fair severance. The VP did not like that these women trusted me, and I became her target once the severance agreements were signed. She did not understand that if I had not met with them, she would have been named in a lawsuit. When I would speak in meetings, she would start on her Blackberry to the VP of Sales. I could tell she was talking about me because of how he looked when her message was read. She managed to get rid of me because I missed an important deadline but called it a Reduction in Force. She put her family member in the position I held as Director of HR with no experience and gave it a different title so that I could not sue her.

I have learned that I have to stand up for what is right, even if I am standing alone, and I would be doing a disservice to the organizations and the very bosses that were targeting me by not telling them the truth despite the cost to me.

Time to Reflect

- Have you had to stand up for something, and no one supported you, but you knew you were right?

- Have you witnessed senior managers misbehaving?

- What does your organization need to be honest about?

- Have you experienced a Human Resources Department or manager that did not seem to care about the employees? How did it make you feel?

Chapter 8

Organizational Observations

I began observing cultures about thirty years ago. I often felt I was the only one or at least one of very few who did not like what I was experiencing in the workplace. Over the years, I have met plenty of people, just like me, that do not thrive in negative atmospheres. I wrote this in 1997 and expounded on it in this book. It is titled "New in a Corporate Job."

NEW IN A CORPORATE JOB

<u>*Acclimating*</u>

Being the new person in a corporate job, in and of itself is difficult. You already have these feelings of anxiety because you are concerned with doing a good job, liking your co-workers, and having a fair boss. Unfortunately, most companies treat new employees like outsiders. Current employees complain about managing their workload, but when management brings in new employees to alleviate their complaints, they treat them as outsiders. They do not want to train them, especially if the new employee is at a higher level in compensation. What is really sad is that most employees have no intention of treating new people like outsiders (unless they are disgruntled). They just seem to forget what it is like to be the new person and how they felt when people treated them. **(Human nature is weird.)**

Policies vs. culture

Acclimating into a new culture does not seem like it should be difficult, but most of the time, it is. All these silent rules are displayed by the behavior of the employees even though the written company values, vision, and policies state differently. For example, most companies (at least the ones worth anything) have guidelines on equal employment opportunity and ethics on treating people in the workplace. These policies state that the company will not tolerate discrimination or harassment and usually offer ways for employees to deal with these things should they encounter them. For example, a complaint procedure or grievance process. However, I have found, in most cases, that the people handling the employee issues (usually HR) do the following:

- *Have an allegiance to support management only (it may not be written, but it is undoubtedly displayed*

in their actions or lack thereof).
- Have an allegiance to support only people that are like them (white, male, or whatever the dominant dynamic is).
- Covering up or sugar-coating wrongdoing instead of dealing with it because the person may be a part of the two mentioned above.
- Doing nothing about the issue, hoping it will just go away (too afraid to speak up).
- Labeling people that complain "troublemakers," even though they have a valid or legal complaint.
- Supporting management recommendations to get rid of the "troublemakers" (retaliation).

I joined the Human Resources Profession because of the integrity that is supposed to be possessed by HR Professionals. I have witnessed HR Vice Presidents, Directors, and Managers not standing for integrity at all, but instead, they partner with management to execute their agendas, no matter how wrong they are. **(And we wonder why no one trusts Human Resources).**

I have personally experienced discrimination and hostility in the workplace as an African American female. In some of my previous workplaces, the dominant culture (usually white males and females) has been <u>allowed</u> to treat me like Affirmative Action was the reason I was hired and that I should just be grateful that I have a job. Instead, they look *at my brown skin and make their own assumptions, usually not good ones. They seem APPALLED when I have an opinion; SURPRISED when they realize I have intelligence; CONCERNED when they recognize how intelligent I am, and ANGRY when they feel I have become their competition or problem.* ***(The nerve of some people!)***

Company policies, in my opinion, are written to make employees think that the company is doing the things that these policies say they are doing. Still, the true determinant of culture is the behavior of the employees, not the policies. For instance, if a policy states, "We value our employees; therefore, they need to balance work and family," Meaning, they should be offered flexible working hours, have manageable workloads to avoid burnout, and company-sponsored programs to keep employees with a healthy mind, body, and spirit (EAP's, health and fitness programs). Instead, employees are overworked, don't have time for health and fitness because they are always at work, and have early morning or late day meetings put on their calendar, thereby invalidating the flexible hours. The unhealthy mind, body, and spirit result from witnessing bad things in the workplace, resenting their job for taking away everything that matters to them (family time, recreation), or just being stressed out! ***(Where is the balance here?)***

Another policy that gets me is the liberal PTO (paid time off) benefit they never intend for you to use. If you do, you will indeed be looked upon as a bad employee who does not have any initiative. Of course, I understand that some people abuse time off, but why have the benefit in writing if your real expectation is to have employees working as much as possible and only grant them time off when they are at the point of burnout?

With all of this, a new employee walks in the door with expectations based on the values, vision, and mission statements, but instead, they witness the actual culture and are dismayed. Consequently, this dream job suddenly turns into just another mundane job that de-energizes and devalues the new employee, thereby not getting maximum productivity from them. Not to mention a higher rate of turnover, employee relations issues, and absenteeism. ***(You have wasted your time and effort bringing them in).***

Diversity

Diversity programs, in most organizations, are just buzzwords. Most company's diversity efforts are limited to hiring visible minorities or women to make it look like they are progressive. No wonder most people feel that diversity is just the new name for Affirmative Action. Most employees, especially those of the dominant culture, have bad taste in their mouths whenever the word "diversity" is mentioned and do not feel they have anything to gain from diversity. This is unfortunate because diversity is all-inclusive. It is also sad because by limiting diversity efforts to recruitment only, the organization has failed to consider how they will retain the diverse employees. You open yourself and your organization up for scrutiny when you have a high turnover of minorities and women.

Before companies create diversity initiatives, they need to know the actual goal and if their managers (senior, middle, and frontline) will genuinely support it. It needs to be demonstrated from the top down, and funding needs to be allocated for training and education in diversity.

I have witnessed companies with diversity programs, initiatives, and councils but the culture is not changing. Granted, most employees understand that they will have people of different genders and cultures working with them (that is what affirmative action is for, right?). But, still, their expectation is that these people come in and assimilate into the dominant culture's way of doing things. In other words, the "group think approach," or whatever you wish to call it, is the expectation, and you have a bunch of Stepford Wives running around without an original idea in their heads because the employees have not been allowed to think for themselves. **(Where is the value in that?)**

<u>Tenure</u>

This is an interesting topic because I have learned that there are advantages and disadvantages to high and low tenure. For the sake of simplicity, I will tell you what I mean by high and low tenure.

- *High tenure – a company with minimal turnover; where employees have been there for a long time (average 5 years or more); people expect to retire from the company; promotion from within has been the norm and is usually seniority-based.*

- *Low tenure – a company with high turnover; employees are there for little time (average less than 5 years); people have no expectation of retiring from the company; promotion is based on being patient enough to wait on others to leave.*

Most high tenure organizations have a paternalistic culture because they are used to taking care of their own. These organizations are usually stable and have experienced minimal change, and employees stay because they are comfortable and become complacent. When the organization begins to experience the difference, the employees complain and resist the change. Their mentality is, "we've always done it this way, so why do we have to change now." Not realizing that several organizations experience change constantly. For example, telecommunications or banking. These organizations suffer because employee morale drops, productivity drops, the rumor-mill runs rampant, absenteeism increases, and the bottom line is affected. At this point, employees are staying because they do not want to lose their pensions. Their attitude reflects this, and they are of no value to the organization. **(Is a new employee going to feel welcomed here?)**

Low-tenure organizations experience the opposite. Employees are usually not loyal because they do not see the company taking care of anyone. The turnover rate is high, benefits are generally minimal, and the salary is not competitive enough to handcuff the employee. These organizations are changing all of the time because they are just trying to find ways to get the work done, retain employees, and reduce risks (losing customers and having lawsuits). The bottom line is affected, and quality is suffering. **(No corporation is gaining anything from this!)**

Generation Gaps
It is difficult to imagine that age differences cause conflict amongst employees, but it does. Employees from the Baby Boomer generation (born 1946ish – 1960ish) have different thoughts about work ethic than Generation X-ers (born 1961-ish – 1980-ish). Baby Boomers seem to think that putting their job first is essential and that experience is valued over education. Whereas Generation X-ers are genuinely looking for that balance between work and family and believe that education should hold its weight when hiring and promotion decisions are made. Differences of opinion, like these, certainly cause conflict in the workplace. Not to mention the difference in work styles, attitudes, thought processes, fashion styles, and other elements. All of these

differences are colliding and causing conflict at work. There are also two other generations present in the workplace, the Veterans, and the Millennials, who also have distinct traits and work ethics, which means, more conflict!

WHERE ORGANIZATIONS NEED TO BE
Acclimating

Take time to train new employees. It does not matter what kind of experience or education they walk in the door with. They still need to be trained on your organization's processes. This will ensure that the new employee is learning correctly and sharing the workload with other employees. In addition, it will get the new employee up to speed quickly and with more confidence. Instead of having them search for every ounce of information they can find; and possibly burning them out before they benefit the organization.

Policies vs. culture

Work hard to have your culture congruent with your policies. If you have a policy (vision statement, value statement, ethics statement) follow it. For example, allow employees to be able to use their time off without repercussion. Make sure that employees are hired and promoted for the right reasons. And by all means, when you witness an employee out of line (It should not matter how long they have been with the company or what position they hold) ... DEAL WITH THEM! Especially if it is something that could lead to legal problems or violence.

Diversity
If you have diversity programs or initiatives, make sure you walk the talk. Understand diversity, embrace it, educate the entire organization, tie the initiatives to performance evaluations and hold people accountable. Create an environment of inclusion, make people feel welcomed, try to understand their uniqueness, respect who they are, and allow them to bring ideas and creativity to the environment and the job you hired them to do. Do not expect them to act like, look like, dress like, or think like you or anyone else.

Tenure
Companies need a mix of high and low tenure to avoid the disadvantages of being on extreme ends of the pendulum. High-tenured employees bring a wealth of historical knowledge that can keep an organization from making huge mistakes and setting new precedents (that could lead to lawsuits). Low-tenured employees bring the value of new ideas and experiences from other organizations that can keep companies from bumping their head against the wall and ultimately saving them money. With these combined, you get the tenure in the middle of the scale where it needs to be.

Generation Gaps
It is essential to understand that the attitude of your co-workers toward their job is not the same as yours. Do what works for you and at the same time allow them to do what works for them. Do not treat people like they are

beneath you if they have not put in 10 or more years in the workforce. Remember, they spent many years in classrooms, libraries, and study groups. At the same time, do not treat people like their experience does not measure up to your college degrees or certifications. Remember, it was their dedication and endurance that kept that organization functioning for many years. We must learn to bridge the gaps in the generations and seek to respect our co-workers a little better.

I did not realize in 1997 that this disdain I was feeling would birth this book many years later. I just knew things were not right, and I did not like the behavior of people in organizations especially those in management roles.

Time to Reflect

- Can you define your workplace culture?

- Is your culture positive or negative? Why?

- Is your workplace culture a reflection of the written words on your Mission, Vision, and Values Statements?

- Have you been in a workplace that seemed to go against your morals and values? How did it make you feel?

- Has the workplace experience made you feel like you are doing God's work? If so, define it.

Chapter 9

What Guides You?

I am not saying that every organization is dysfunctional, but people can be. The more people an organization has, the more problems it will contend with. People create atmospheres and cultures. We talk a good game from city to city, corporation to corporation, and entity to entity. But seriously, who truly stands for the things they claim to stand for? How many people would hold their senior managers accountable?

I have met so many people who are unaware of themselves and refuse to model the appropriate behaviors. They think they are great leaders when, in fact, they are not leaders at all; they are not even good managers. They believe that they are something special because, on paper, everything looks good, and the bottom-line results are what the organization cares about. However, if you look deeper into the turnover, employee complaints, absenteeism, or illnesses in their departments and then measure those results against the bottom line, you will have a different perspective, an accurate picture of who that manager really is. They think that people like and respect them, but most people find them detestable; they confuse fear with respect. They believe that they have earned some level of prestige in high-level positions when their role has made their lack of empathy or humility more visible.

True leaders understand and embrace the ability to mentor, train, listen, serve, grow, and take all of their experiences and learnings to the next level. True leaders have a solid moral compass that leads them and their actions. A moral compass, as defined by Oxford Languages, is "a person's ability to judge what is right and wrong and to act accordingly." Moral compasses are guiding principles that we use to make decisions and govern our actions and are usually developed from the things we have been taught as children. Here are some questions to ask yourself to determine where you stand as it relates to morals:

- Did you have a family that believed in Godly principles?

- Were you corrected when you were wrong?

- Did your parents discipline you to teach you consequences?

- Were you allowed to think for yourself and give a

little latitude to make small mistakes so that you would avoid huge ones?

- Did you learn to share and play nice with other children?

- Were you expected to be polite and kind to everyone?

- Were you taught that you are not superior to anyone and that everyone you encounter has a story?

- Have you been taught that people's handicaps and disabilities are not a laughing matter?

- Were you taught to respect authority?

- Were you taught to voice your concerns respectfully?

- Were you taught to be responsible for the things you own?

- Were you taught to be honest and accountable?

Moral compasses are teachings that we embrace also. If we decide to ignore all the wisdom planted in us and embrace harmful teachings or even dark practices, we will have a different moral compass than those who embrace good things and Christian principles.

Moral compasses can also be developed through trauma. Yes, trauma. When people experience trauma, they are forced to see life differently. Sometimes our most remarkable growth comes from situations that make us extremely uncomfortable. For example, the death of our loved ones makes us appreciate life or at least think about it. Pain, betrayal, and a broken heart make us remember when things were good and force us to look at life differently.

Time to Reflect

- What are your morals or guiding principles?
- Do you have some principles that need to change?
- Have your morals changed throughout your life? If so, what caused them to change?
- What are characteristics you value?

Chapter 10

Dealing with The Root Cause, Not the Manifestation

Many of us live our lives trying to get away from or overcompensate for something that did or did not happen when we were young. For instance, growing up in a home where there was financial struggle, I ended up with a boyfriend who made money in a very questionable way. He provided me with money and helped contribute toward my financial well-being, but at that early age I did not realize that his showering me with money and gifts was a set-up from Satan for me to resent experiencing struggle and to create a path for me to chase money. From this experience alone, I had a skewed view of how money was to be handled. I would get it and spend it as soon as it hit my pocket because I was accustomed to more coming and not being in a position of having to budget or handle money God's way. When the money ran out, I spent many years trying to mask my pain to the outside world. I was well-groomed and dressed nice, but I was broke. I had no money management skills and detested the thought of a budget. I even hated playing Monopoly because it was too much like real life and made me have the same feelings of anger and resentment when I lost properties, money, was derailed (taken backwards) or thrown in jail. I realize that is silly, but it truly was how I felt about that game, and I was annoyed that it was made.

The manifestation I displayed was not truly the root cause. I showed manifestations of a prosperous life, but the root cause was resentment of struggle that Satan planted in me. These two things were complete opposite of one another. So, this lifestyle of trying to avoid the root cause resulted in me getting into a lot of debt. Credit cards, pay day loans, and personal loans. I filed bankruptcy twice and still did not embrace the budgeting and financial management classes given to me because I was still harboring resentment. I needed to deal with the root cause and fertilize it to embrace the proper skills being granted to me. God, being the Abba Father He is, would not let me continue on this journey of a fruitless life without taking me back to the source of my resentment and pain. The resentment of struggle and obtaining things the right way, the longer way, and what was seemingly the harder way did not make me feel good. I had to ask who was my resentment toward and why was I embarrassed about some of the things from my childhood?

Dealing With The Root Cause, Not The Manifestation

God took me back into my past and I learned that when my stepdad lost his job and experienced the DT's, I went into protection mode to keep people from knowing the truth that our family was in a crisis. I was not old enough or smart enough to know what to do to fix the crisis, after all, that was my parent's job. However, I felt the need to create lies and wear masks that I believed would hide the problems we were experiencing and to embrace a man that made money look like it was easy to obtain. I went to school every day for years and maintained good grades in both high school and college. But when life happened and things got rough, I experienced stress to the point where I would be anxious, lose weight and my hair would fall out. I would borrow money to keep up the façade and get into more debt, stress, and anxiety. I did not realize that I was creating the very reality I ran from so long ago. In other words, my manifestation had a "Come to Jesus" meeting with my root cause. I had to learn to embrace a budget and live within my means. I also learned that this was the root cause of the pride issues God had me to deal with. Pride can manifest in many ways, but there is always a root cause (a source).

Have you ever seen a plant that once thrived and then started to wither away? You see the plant go from budding to dying. You remove the dead leaves and debris and add water, but the plant still continues to die. You put it in a different place where it gets more natural sunlight, but it still is stagnant and dying slowly. You then buy new potting soil and fertilizer, and you replant it in this new soil. All of a sudden, the plant seems happy and starts thriving again. Well, all of this to say, the characters and personalities I have encountered in the workforce have a story; a situation that defined their character and behavior. They must have that epiphany, just like I did to deal with the root cause. The only thing that can change behavior is to deal with the root cause. The old soil has lost its nutrients and is full of dead things like dried roots, debris, and dust. This old soil provides nothing for the root to draw from to continue its growth. The newly fertilized soil is rich in nutrients and other good things that aid in supporting the stability and growth of the plant. The newly fertilized soil is also free of dead things that will drain the plant starting at its root.

Just to be clear, no one is exempt from pain, embarrassment or situations that will make us uncomfortable or change the trajectory of our lives. It does not matter if you were born privileged or unprivileged or into a two-parent home or a single-parent home. God is no respecter of persons and does not care about our comfort, He cares about our character. He will use the most uncomfortable situations in our lives to build character or allow us to become extremely uncomfortable in situations where the purpose He ordained is fulfilled. His goal is to ultimately lead us to our divine purpose in life, but we must be willing participants. He does not want these uncomfortable situations to sift us like wheat, but He will allow the sifting to separate the wheat from the tares. He also allows us to go through things to be a testimony that will help other people. He uses everything, good and bad, and makes it work for His glory.

We cannot truly help people until we have been through some things ourselves and newly fertilized soil (a renewed mind) is required for us to stop a negative path and to move into a positive one. We cannot change our behaviors without changing our mindsets. In order to change our minds, we have to recognize that there is a problem with our behavior. Eventually, all bad behavior will bring us to some uncomfortable places and prove there is a need for a change. Let us face it, if we could just press a "change behavior" button we would have taken the easy road and done that, right? So, when we come to the place where we realize we are living the definition of insanity (doing the same things, the same way over and over, but expecting different results) we will be forced to make a change or justify why everyone else is the problem and not ourselves. Unfortunately, most will justify and blame shift because they do not want to believe they have a problem and need to change. But this book is for the few of us who realize justifying is just lying to ourselves and is a deeper definition of insanity.

He also spoke this parable: A certain man had a fig tree planted in his vineyard, and he came seeking fruit on it and found none. Then he said to the keeper of his vineyard, "Look, for three years I have come seeking fruit on this fig tree and find none. Cut it down; why does is use up the ground?" But he answered and said to him, "Sir, let it alone this year also, until I dig around it and fertilize it. And if it bears fruit, well. But if not, after that you can cut it down." Luke 13: 6-9 NKJV

I feel extremely fortunate to serve a God who is like the Keeper of the Vineyard. He wants to fertilize us with his Word, the bread of life, and give us the opportunity to bear the right fruit, kill unhealthy root causes and be replanted on fertile soil.

Time to Reflect

- Have you experienced any habits or strongholds in your life? Have you conquered them?

- Do you have experiences (root causes) that you have not truly dealt with and given to God?

- Have you gone through some difficult experiences and could not understand why God allowed these things?

Summary

Workplaces are just brick and mortar buildings, and they are not bad, but people create culture. People are complex beings that encompass body, mind, and spirit. Their experiences have created spiritual anemia in some areas that has resulted from traumas, upbringing, failures, and the like. No one wears a sign on them that says, "I'm delicate from betrayal," "I'm calloused from hurt," or "I'm competitive because I'm insecure." But it comes out in their character and behavior.

With every experience, we can choose to become better or bitter. Those are the infamous words of T.D. Jakes. Granted, this is easier said than done in some situations. If we look for good in every experience, no matter how bad it seems, we will become better from the experience opposed to bitter about it. We become what we embrace. If Paul the Apostle kept focusing and complaining about the thorn in his side, he would not have accepted that God's grace was sufficient for him. He would have missed his destiny focusing on his thorn.

Playground Personalities

I once read something that said, "people don't leave jobs, they leave bosses." I agree with this, but will take it a step further and say, "people don't leave jobs, they leave the culture." The boss is not always the problem, but if the boss is not willing to deal with the problem child or children they still contribute to the problem.

It is truly NOT ABOUT US! We are to serve people. Servanthood is a responsibility and a privilege of a leader, not just a position. We must learn that offense, arrogance, pride, and ego are all killers of our ability to grow. If we never acknowledge our limitations and feel that we have no room for growth we do not evolve and what does not evolve becomes extinct.

I encourage you to take time to put mobile devices down and engage in conversation with the person next to you on the train, the bus, in the airport, on the elevator, or wherever you encounter people. Wisdom and growth come from embracing other human experiences despite their age, their social economic status, their race, or anything that makes them unique.

Wisdom also comes from being real about who we are and where we fall short. Needing God's help does not make us weak; it makes us strong. By making a concerted effort to acknowledge and work on our own shortcomings and being willing to take constructive criticism makes us better

Summary

and keeps us growing. We all have growth opportunities that require a commitment to change the things about ourselves that need to be changed. We cannot control others, but we can control how we perceive, process, and respond to people, situations, and circumstances.

Let us make the world a better place by allowing change to begin with us and to consistently grow and improve over time.

Final Word

One day in 2002, I asked God to let me be comfortable and to let me go into a workplace to be stable and to get a steady paycheck. The Holy Spirit spoke to me and said, "Since when have you been comfortable and when have you had a steady paycheck?" I responded and said, "Never. This is why I am making this statement." God responded and said, "I have put a fight in your belly because you are supposed to stand against injustice. You will encounter people you feel are giants based on their dispositions and positions, but I am with you and will guide you through these battles."

God gave me the title and the inspiration to write this book in 2008, although it was being birthed in me eleven years prior. This book has taken me years to complete because I had to live through the events. Most feel that ministry is only in a church, but that is far from the truth. I have been used as a minister, a missionary, a prophet, counselor, coach, and prayer warrior in the corporate arena. God has taken me from Kansas City, MO to several cities and workplaces to learn that culture is real, people are hurting, and

Playground Personalities

Satan is busy. I have been blessed to meet some phenomenal people along the way; people who needed God's protection and a vessel to deliver messages. On the flip side, I have also met some pretty rotten characters. But nothing is in vain, as those rotten characters taught me some unbelievably valuable lessons in what not to be.

It has not been easy, nor has it been my desire to move at times God was calling me away from a workplace or a city. I have been in some positions I really liked. There was a time I did not obey and move because the money was good, and I was well respected in that workplace. God allowed me to get extremely uncomfortable in the very environment I once thrived in. He was even gracious enough to send a Prophetess to tell me I was late for an assignment and that I was going to a place to deal with an extraordinarily strong demonic force. I argued with her and told her she was wrong and told her my plans. She laughed and said, you are not going where you think you are and there have been some conversations at high levels about you. The very next day, I was called into a meeting with my General Manager and a field HR President who was three-levels higher than me. I was told that I was being moved to a position I did not apply for and that they were doing this because they did not want to see my talent leave the organization. I could not continue to be rebellious to God, so I took the assignment and surely faced one of the strongest Goliaths I have encountered thus far.

Final Word

I have also found myself going through what I call "Joseph experiences." I have had times that I was doing very well financially and put in very high-ranking positions. I was taken from those situations when I least expected and found myself in some very awkward places. I have been flat broke and homeless, but during those times I experienced God's sustainment. He gave me manna, but I was far from the land of milk & honey. I have always been and continue to be amazed at how God will show me He is with me, sustaining me in the midst of being forced out of a place like Joseph was when his jealous brothers sold him into slavery or what may seem like an unfair stay in prison like Joseph experienced when he refused to sleep with Potiphar's wife and was lied on. Although I did not actually experience prison or jail, I have experienced feeling alone, uncomfortable under the "house rules" of other people.

I am sure you are probably thinking, "If she is God's child, why did He allow her to suffer financially and be homeless?" I am glad you ask and here is the short story. I had a fourteen-year period where I was married and financially stable. During that time, I was growing in my faith and in the Word of God. I had abundance and most people coveted my lifestyle. I would give people the clothes off of my back and there did not seem to be very much I would not do to help someone. But something was wrong; God told me I was full of pride. This confused me greatly because how can I be full of pride when I would help anyone. God told me, that I was so prideful I would not allow anyone to help me. I said, but I do not need help. A couple of days after that conversation with God, I was hanging out with a close friend who wanted to ride with me while I went shopping for household items. We passed by a Dollar General and she asked me why I did not stop there first opposed to heading to Target. I told her, in a very arrogant manner, that Dollar General was for poor people, and I would not be caught shopping there. When I saw her facial expression and disdain toward my comment, I tried to justify it by saying that I felt stores like that were for people who are really struggling, and I would be wrong for taking things they need. Pride and arrogance are filled with justifying behaviors.

Shortly after that statement my fourteen-year marriage came to an end, I found myself so completely depressed that I could not make a decision. I lost my job due to depression, a missed deadline, and a battle with a VP for standing up for the rights of others (I mentioned this earlier). I spent five months literally sleeping and seeing a mental health professional. When my unemployment ran out, I moved away because I could not find a job. There were times I did not even have enough money to catch the train home from work and God would send a beautiful stranger to step in to pay my fare without question or wanting anything in return. I had a friend who allowed me to crash on a cot in her basement for two months and pay her a small amount. I still had to pay on my apartment in Kansas City so that I

Final Word

would not have a broken lease on my credit. Once my lease was fulfilled, I moved into my own place in Chicago. I had friends who were nice enough to loan me money when I would humble myself and ask. I had to sell my Mercedes and get a Hyundai because I could not afford the repairs on it. I lost so many material things during this time.

God could not use me when I was full of pride. He had to allow me to be uncomfortable and in need to understand how humiliating it is to have to ask someone for help. He also had to show me how nasty people could be when you needed them. I had many friends when I had money to blow, but when I needed them, most ran away and looked down on me because I was no longer someone, they could be proud of. These experiences taught me quite a bit. I learned that every friendship has one of three purposes.

1. The Receiver. You are put there to assist them in some way. You act as a mentor or witness to them. They see you as their rock and they do not want you to be weak or unsteady in any way. When you are going through something, this person will never be there for you. When you try to talk to them about things you are going through, they will brush you off and say something like, "You'll get through it. You are strong."

2. The Giver. They are there to assist you in some way.

> This person will be a witness or a mentor to you. They will come into your life, for a period of time, and give you some nuggets of wisdom to take with you on your journey. They may even be there to help you out of a bad situation. These people will give you advice but do not expect them to receive it from you. They came to give and that is their role.
>
> 3. The Reciprocator. You will assist each other and reciprocate support, care, and concern. These people are usually in your life for the long haul. They love you when you are strong and when you are weak. Unfortunately, this list of people will be really short.

I learned not to cast someone in a role they were never capable of playing in my life. With every friendship, I ask God the purpose of this person in my life. Keep people in the role they are meant to play and do not expect anything else from them. I can write another entire book on that subject, but for the purpose of bringing this book to a close I will state that God had a lot to teach me and that I had to go through and grow through so many obstacles. I am grateful for all of them and know there will be many more as I am continuously being refined.

The greatest lesson I have learned is that I need God and can trust Him. He revealed to me that I could not see him as a loving father who really wanted to give me his best because I did not have that in an earthly father. God had me write down

Final Word

all the attributes I admired of the fathers I had observed over the years. I told God I admired fathers who protect their families, are faithful to them and make their needs as a priority, teach their children how to be upright citizens with Godly character, recognize and develop the innate talents of their children, push their children to greatness opposed to limiting their dreams, and make sure their family has everything they need. God simplified this and said, you admire supporters, protectors, and providers. I am all of these things and much more. You have to believe I am your father.

"For I know the plans I have for you," declares the Lord, "plans to prosper you and not to harm you, plans to give you hope and a future." Jeremiah 29:11

Thank you for taking time to read this book. It is my belief is that our heavenly father will put this book in the hands of the right people, at the right time and for the right reasons. I pray that the observations and lessons will be testimonies for someone else experiencing the nuances of ministry outside of the four walls of the church. I want you to know, you are making a difference.

Many blessings and many thanks.

Dorice Woodruff

CPSIA information can be obtained
at www.ICGtesting.com
Printed in the USA
LVHW050357020222
709976LV00014B/672